THE PROTOEVANGELIUM OF JAMES

Greek and English Texts

Translated by: Alexander Walker

Commentary by: D.P. Curtin

Illustrations by: Albrecht Durer

Dalcassian Publishing Co.

Philadelphia, PA

THE PROTOEVANGELIUM OF JAMES

Library of Congress Cataloging-in-Publication Data

Copyright © 2019 Dalcassian Publishing Co.
In association with St. Macartan Press
All rights reserved.

THE PROTOEVANGELIUM OF JAMES

FORWARD

The Protoevangelium Jacobi, or Infancy Gospel of James

It purports to have been written by "James the brother of the Lord", i.e. the Apostle James the Less. It is based on the canonical Gospels which it expands with legendary and imaginative elements, which are sometimes puerile or fantastic. The birth, education, and marriage of the Blessed Virgin are described in the first eleven chapters and these are the source of various traditions current among the faithful. They are of value in indicating the veneration paid to Mary at a very early age. For instance it is the "Protoevangelium" which first tells that Mary was the miraculous offspring of Joachim and Anna, previously childless; that when three years old the child was taken to the Temple and dedicated to its service, in fulfilment of her parents' vow. When Mary was twelve Joseph is chosen by the high-priest as her spouse in obedience to a miraculous sign — a dove coming out of his rod and resting on his head. The nativity is embellished in an unrestrained manner. Critics find that the "Protoevangelium" is a composite into which two or three documents enter. It was known to Origen under the name of the "Book of James". There are signs in St. Justin's works that he was acquainted with it, or at least with a parallel tradition. The work, therefore, has been ascribed to the second century. Portions of it show a familiarity with Jewish customs, and critics have surmised that the groundwork was composed by a Jewish-Christian. The "Protoevangelium" exists in ancient Greek and Syriac recensions. There are also Armenian and Latin translations.

The Birth of Mary the Holy Mother of God, and Very Glorious Mother of Jesus Christ.

CHAPTER I

1:1   In the records of the twelve tribes of Israel was Joachim[1], a man rich exceedingly;

1:2   and he brought his offerings double[2], saying: "There shall be of my superabundance to all the people, and there shall be the

---

[1] Joachim appears to be also universally accepted as the name of the father of Mary going back to the early 2nd century. The only known exception in the Nestorian Bishop Solomon of Basrah, who claims that her father was Zadok ben Jotham, grandson of a certain Mattan (*Book of the Bee, 33*). While the two former names are unparalleled in Davidic genealogies, the name Mattan appears to be recurrent in both the Luke and Matthew's Gospel, as well as in various traditions. Additionally, rabbinical sources in the Abarabanel genealogy mention a certain Mattan ben Eliab, a patrilineal Davidic descendent, residing around the 1st century BC.

offering for my forgiveness to the Lord for a propitiation for me[3]."

1:3 For the great day of the Lord was at hand, and the sons of Israel were bringing their offerings[4].

1:4 And there stood over against him Rubim[5], saying: "It is not meet for you first to bring your offerings, because you have not made seed in Israel."

1:5 And Joachim was exceedingly grieved, and went away to the registers of the twelve tribes of the people, saying: "I shall see the registers of the twelve tribes of Israel[6], as to whether I alone have not made seed in Israel."

1:6 And he searched and found that all the righteous had raised up seed in Israel.

1:7 And he called to mind the patriarch Abraham, that in the last day God gave him a son Isaac.

1:8 And Joachim was exceedingly grieved, and did not come into the presence of his wife;[7]

1:9 but he retired to the desert[8], and there pitched his tent, and fasted forty days and forty nights[9], saying in himself: "I will not

---

[2] Faustus, the famous 4th century Manichean and contemporary of St. Augustine claimed that Joachim was of the tribe of Levi, as a means of explaining his right to render animal sacrifices. Augustine refutes this in his famous case against the Manicheans (*Contra Faustum, 23.4*)

[3] The author here appears to be referencing the Jewish feast of atonement, best known as Yom Kippur (Lev. 16:1-34, 23:26-32; Num. 29:7-11).

[4] Curiously, while the ritual animal sacrifice is highlighted by the author(s), references to the city of Jerusalem as the cultic center of this practice are limited in this text. This might be a function of the assumed association between ritual practice and the temple site; or alternatively, as an intentional measure by the author to demote the importance and validity of the priestly administration in Jerusalem.

[5] This appears to be a member of the Jerusalem priesthood, who lays claims that Joachim is in violation of the mitzvah to procreate (Gen. 1:28). The name 'Rubim' is also an anomalous name, as it appears to have no rabbinical or biblical parallel. Alternatively, other manuscripts render this name as Reuban. While some texts claim that this Rubim/Reuban was High Priest, this does not conform to the known Jewish list of High Priests. However, this appears to be a point of confusion with a large body of Christian Apocrypha. Alternatively, the Gospel of the Infancy of Mary notes a certain Issachar in place of Reuban in its narrative.

[6] Josephus recounts that the Jerusalem temple authorities held a repository of the Jewish national genealogies (*Against Apion, 1.7*), which was allegedly destroyed or damaged under the reign of Herod the Great. Joachim's claim to search this archive is plausible, albeit unclear in terms of his motives for doing so.

[7] The Gospel of Pseudo-Matthew recounts similar events are those here, granting a firm chronology of events. It appears that the author of that text employed much of their account upon this work. Pseudo-Matthew states that he was abiding in the wilderness for five months' time.

go down either for food or for drink until the Lord my God shall look upon me, and prayer shall be my food and drink[10]."

---

[8] This retirement to the desert seems pregnant with potential contextual meaning, particularly given the renunciation that Joachim receives previously from the Jerusalem priesthood. It is deeply tempting to associate this time of retreat from the desert with the Essene community which was flourishing in Judea at this time. This is particularly pertinent as it relates to celibacy, regular fasting, and confrontation with the Jerusalem priesthood. However, since Joachim as a figure only appears in Christian hagiography, there is no way of definitively establishing this relationship.

[9] See parallel in Matthew 4:2

[10] This too is a common pious practice during Yom Kippur amongst observant Jews.

CHAPTER II

2:1   And his wife Anna mourned in two mournings, and lamented in two lamentations, saying: "I shall bewail my widowhood[11];

2:2   I shall bewail my childlessness." And the great day of the Lord was at hand;

2:3   and Judith[12] her maid-servant said: "How long do you humiliate your soul?

2:4   Behold, the great day of the Lord is at hand, and it is unlawful for you to mourn[13].

2:5   But take this head-band, which the woman that made it gave to me;

2:6   for it is not proper that I should wear it, because I am a maid-servant, and it has a royal appearance[14]."

2:7   And Anna said: "Depart from me;

2:8   for I have not done such things, and the Lord has brought me very low.

2:9   I fear that some wicked person has given it to you, and you have come to make me a sharer in your sin."

2:10   And Judith said: "Why should I curse you, seeing that the Lord has shut your womb, so as not to give you fruit in Israel?"

2:11   And Anna was grieved exceedingly, and put off her garments of mourning, and cleaned her head, and put on her wedding

---

[11] While her widowhood would be protected by Jewish law (Deut. 26:12; Ex. 22:21), her social status would be greatly reduced regardless of her wealth. Rabbinical tradition advises men to avoid marriage with widows (*Zohar, ii. 102a-b; Pesahim 111a-b*). Further to this same point, it appears there was some concern that widows and/or the childless were a hazard to marry as it was believed that they may have some reproductive disease (*Yevamot, 64b*).

[12] While perhaps a common name of the period, being the feminine variant of Judah. It is also the name render for Joseph the Carpenter's mother in both Syriac (*Cave of Treasures, Conflict of Adam and Eve*) and Ethiopian sources (*Kebra Negast, 70*). The reason why this name is rendered lends credence that the author(s) are alluding to a specific individual known to their audience. The invention of a specific name would serve no purpose to the narrative otherwise.

[13] It is not permissible to mourn or to sit shiva during a major Jewish holiday.

[14] Most likely it was either ornate or a hue of violet, which was only associated with a reigning royal house in the Levantine sphere.

garments, and about the ninth hour[15] went down to the garden to walk.

2:12 And she saw a laurel[16], and sat under it, and prayed to the Lord, saying: "O God of our fathers, bless me and hear my prayer, as You blessed the womb of Sarah, and gave her a son Isaac."[17]

---

[15] A Common hour of Jewish prayer during the Second Temple period (Acts 3:1) known as 'Minchah'. This was often associated with both confession and the offering of gifts, both of which appear to be relevant to the context of Anna's prayer.

[16] The allusion to the Laurel tree here appears intentional, as it is associated with both the Davidic Psalm (Ps. 37:35), as well its botanical properties, as it is a hardy plant and easily propagates.

[17] See parallel in Gen. 21:2

CHAPTER III

3:1 And gazing towards the heaven, she saw a sparrow's nest in the laurel[18], and made a lamentation in herself, saying: "Alas! Who begot me?

3:2 And what womb produced me[19]? Because I have become a curse in the presence of the sons of Israel, and I have been reproached, and they have driven me in derision out of the temple of the Lord[20].

3:3 Alas! To what have I been likened?

3:4 I am not like the fowls of the heaven, because even the fowls of the heaven are productive before You, O Lord.

3:5 Alas! To what have I been likened?

3:6 I am not like the beasts of the earth, because even the beasts of the earth are productive before You, O Lord.

3:7 Alas! To what have I been likened?

3:8 I am not like these waters, because even these waters are productive before You, O Lord.

3:9 Alas! To what have I been likened?

3:10 I am not like this earth, because even the earth brings forth its fruits in season, and blesses You, O Lord."

---

[18] See parallel in Tobit 2:10

[19] There are several accounts within Christian hagiography regarding the nativity of St. Anne. Byzantine sources refer to her mother as 'Miriam', although no original source for this has been determined. The Gospel of Pseudo-Matthew states that her father's name was 'Achar', of the House of David. However, more commonly she is called the daughter of Matthan the priest, a denizen of Jerusalem (*Nicephorus Callistus, Historia Ecclesiastica, 2.3*). The latter tradition appears to be more universally repeated and older than the account of Pseudo-Matthew. The association with the House of David appears to be strong in all sources, but its specification appears to vary from source to source.

[20] Again, this seems to curiously parallel the confrontation that Joachim appears to have experienced with the Jerusalem priesthood two chapters prior. It is additionally peculiar as women do not have much interface with the Jewish priesthood, as they were unable to enter the inner courts to observe ritual sacrifice.

CHAPTER IV

4:1 And, behold, an angel of the Lord stood by[21], saying: "Anna, Anna, the Lord has heard your prayer, and you shall conceive, and shall bring forth;

4:2 and your seed shall be spoken of in all the world."

4:3 And Anna said: "As the Lord my God lives, if I beget either male or female, I will bring it as a gift to the Lord my God;

4:4 and it shall minister to Him in holy things all the days of its life[22]."

4:5 And, behold, two angels came, saying to her: "Behold, Joachim your husband is coming with his flocks[23]."

4:6 For an angel of the Lord went down to him[24], saying: "Joachim, Joachim, the Lord God has heard your prayer.

4:7 Go down hence; for, behold, your wife Anna shall conceive."

4:8 And Joachim went down and called his shepherds, saying: "Bring me hither ten she-lambs without spot or blemish, and they shall be for the Lord my God;

4:9 and bring me twelve tender calves, and they shall be for the priests and the elders; and a hundred goats for all the people.[25]"

4:10 And, behold, Joachim came with his flocks;

4:11 and Anna stood by the gate, and saw Joachim coming, and she ran and hung upon his neck, saying: "Now I know that the Lord God has blessed me exceedingly;

4:12 for, behold the widow no longer a widow, and I the childless shall conceive.

4:13 And Joachim rested the first day in his house."

---

[21] The later Gospel of Pseudo-Matthew records this place as being at the gate called 'golden'. This is a well-known place (Acts 3:2) would place the annunciation of Mary at the Temple in Jerusalem, and not at her residence in Sepphoris. Josephus also mentions it in the context of the Kendron Valley.

[22] See 1 Samuel 1:11

[23] This identification of Joachim as a master of various flocks of sheep is also repeated in the Gospel of Pseudo-Matthew.

[24] This is telling statement to the editorial history of this text. Namely because no angel appears to Joachim in this narrative, nor does it appear in any textual variance of this Gospel in any known text. It must have been redacted sometime in antiquity. The reasons for this removal are impossible to discern, and all philological arguments to be made are *ex nihilo* for this reason. An address to Joachim by an angel appears elsewhere in the Infancy Gospel of Mary.

[25] See Ps. 116:17

CHAPTER V

5:1 And on the following day he brought his offerings, saying in himself: "If the Lord God has been rendered gracious to me, the plate on the priest's forehead will make it manifest to me."

5:2 And Joachim brought his offerings, and observed attentively the priest's plate[26] when he went up to the altar of the Lord, and he saw no sin in himself.

5:3 And Joachim said: "Now I know that the Lord has been gracious unto me, and has remitted all my sins."

5:4 And he went down from the temple of the Lord justified and departed to his own house.

5:5 And her months were fulfilled, and in the ninth month Anna brought forth.

5:6 And she said to the midwife: "What have I brought forth?"

5:7 And she said: "A girl."

5:8 And said Anna: "My soul has been magnified this day."

5:9 And she laid her down.

5:10 And the days having been fulfilled[27], Anna was purified, and gave the breast to the child, and called her name 'Mary'.

---

[26] This is a ritual object worn on the forehead of the High Priest (Ex. 28:36). Its exact purpose is disputed.

[27] Under Jewish law, women are defiled for eight days following the birth of their child (Lev. 12:2-7).

CHAPTER VI

6:1   And the child grew strong day by day; and when she was six months old, her mother set her on the ground to try whether she could stand, and she walked seven steps and came into her bosom;

6:2   and she snatched her up, saying: "As the Lord my God lives, you shall not walk on this earth until I bring you into the temple of the Lord."

6:3   And she made a sanctuary in her bedchamber and allowed nothing common or unclean to pass through her.

6:4   And she called the undefiled daughters of the Hebrews[28], and they led her astray.

6:5   And when she was a year old, Joachim made a great feast[29], and invited the priests, and the scribes, and the elders, and all the people of Israel.

6:6   And Joachim brought the child to the priests; and they blessed her, saying: "O God of our fathers, bless this child, and give her an everlasting name to be named in all generations."

6:7   And all the people said: "So be it, so be it, amen."

6:8   And he brought her to the chief priests; and they blessed her, saying: "O God most high, look upon this child, and bless her with the utmost blessing, which shall be forever."

6:9   And her mother snatched her up and took her into the sanctuary of her bedchamber and gave her the breast.

6:10   And Anna made a song to the Lord God, saying: "I will sing a song[30] to the Lord my God, for He has looked upon me, and has taken away the reproach of mine enemies[31];

6:11   and the Lord has given the fruit of His righteousness, singular in its kind, and richly endowed before Him.

6:12   Who will tell the sons of Rubim that Anna gives suck?

6:13   Hear, hear, you twelve tribes of Israel, that Anna gives suck."

6:14   And she laid her to rest in the bedchamber of her sanctuary and went out and ministered unto them.

---

[28] The use of the term 'Hebrews' here grants some insight into the authorship of the text. This word used in the Roman period alluded to Jews who had maintained the common use of the Hebrew language, in contrast to the more common Hellenized Jews who used Greek as their vernacular. There is no common identification of who this group might be, but the association with being 'undefiled' is traditionally associated with sexual purity. The author(s), therefore, must have been Jewish, and held an intimate knowledge of different and competing political groupings within Judaism, but makes no effort to grant them their familiar political name. The reason for this omission is and can only remain speculative.

[29] The traditional accounts of Mary's nativity place her as a resident in the city of Sepphoris, where a large Crusader church still stands, as the alleged site of the familial home. While this is the primary city in the Galilee, its not clear how strong of a tie it would have had with the Herodian or priestly administration in Jerusalem. Assuming the chronology presented here, the birth of Mary would have been around 20 BC, in the midst of Herod the Great's reign.

[30] Most texts say 'new song' which is a common phraseology in biblical Hebrew (Ps. 33:3. 40:3, 144:9, 149:1; Is. 42:10; Rev. 14:3). This occurrence also parallels the events surrounding the birth of Samuel (1 Sam. 2), wherein Hannah gives praise for the birth of her son.

[31] It is unclear who the enemies of Anna are supposed to be. It is possible that part of this narrative was lost or removed from its original form.

6:15 And when the supper was ended, they went down rejoicing, and glorifying the God of Israel.

CHAPTER VII

7:1 And her months were added to the child. And the child was two years old, and Joachim said: "Let us take her up to the temple of the Lord, that we may pay the vow[32] that we have vowed, lest perchance the Lord send to us, and our offering be not received."

7:2 And Anna said: "Let us wait for the third year, in order that the child may not seek for father or mother."

7:3 And Joachim said: "So let us wait."

7:4 And the child was three years old, and Joachim said: "Invite the daughters of the Hebrews that are undefiled, and let them take each a lamp, and let them stand with the lamps burning, that the child may not turn back, and her heart be captivated from the temple of the Lord."

7:5 And they did so until they went up into the temple of the Lord. And the priest[33] received her, and kissed her, and blessed her, saying: "The Lord has magnified your name in all generations. In you, on the last of the days, the Lord will manifest His redemption to the sons of Israel."

7:6 And he set her down upon the third step of the altar[34], and the Lord God sent grace upon her; and she danced with her feet, and all the house of Israel loved her.

---

[32] No vow is referenced in the 'Infancy Gospel of Mary', instead she is brought to the Temple as a matter of education along with other young girls.

[33] Why this priest is left unnamed in the text is peculiar. Since the Jewish temple did not contain vestal virgins as a part of its cultic practice, this 'vow' was likely informal and her residency in the temple was more likely a result of abiding with a priestly relative. Since St. Anne's family is regarded as being of a priestly origin according to Byzantine sources, she may have resided with a maternal uncle or grandfather.

[34] The significance of the third step of the altar is obscure. It clearly holds a ritualistic meaning to the author, which has been lost to history. Pseudo-Matthew says that this took place on the fifteenth step which may be in accord with Psalm 120. Although, the daily functionality of the temple is lost to us currently.

CHAPTER VIII

8:1   And her parents went down marveling, and praising the Lord God, because the child had not turned back[35].

8:2   And Mary was in the temple of the Lord as if she were a dove that dwelt there, and she received food from the hand of an angel[36].

8:3   And when she was twelve years old there was held a council of the priests, saying: "Behold, Mary has reached the age of twelve years in the temple of the Lord.

8:4   What then shall we do with her, lest perchance she defile the sanctuary of the Lord?"[37]

8:5   And they said to the high priest[38]: "You stand by the altar of the Lord;

8:6   go in, and pray concerning her; and whatever the Lord shall manifest unto you, that also will we do."

8:7   And the high priest went in, taking the robe with the twelve bells[39] into the holy of holies;

8:8   and he prayed concerning her.

8:9   And behold an angel of the Lord stood by him, saying unto him: "Zacharias, Zacharias[40], go out and assemble the widowers of the people, and let them bring each his rod;

---

[35] This episode is altogether strange, as no further contact between Mary and her parents appear to exist in any apocryphal works. More to this point, the 'Infancy Gospel of Mary' indicates that she was 'forsaken' by her parents and therefore abandoned to the Jerusalem priesthood. This could imply that they had died in this period. However, there is no tradition that offers clarity on this subject.

[36] This episode is held in high esteem within the liturgical life of the Eastern Orthodox Churches. The Feast of 'The Entry of the Most Holy Theotokos into the Temple' is recounted on November 21st each year with a direct allusion to this occurrence.

[37] This was common ritual practice as menstrual women were deemed to be unclean under Jewish law (Lev. 15:19). Moreover, all those who had contact with her for a seven-day period were also deemed ritually unclean.

[38] The High Priest during this period would have been Simon ben Boethus, who held the office from 23 BC until the death of King Herod in 4BC.

[39] This is a description of the priestly robe of the high priest, also known as the 'robe of the ephod'. It is described in detail in the biblical account (Ex. 28:31-35) but would have been largely unknown to a 2nd century audience, as its utility ended with the destruction of the Jerusalem Temple. The gold bells were an added necessity on Yom Kippur.

[40] There is no high priest recorded as 'Zachariah' in any source. Who the identity of this individual is supposed to be is unclear. While not an uncommon name of this period, no identifiable characteristics are noted by the author(s). This might be a corruption of 'Cantheras' a name associated with Simon ben Boethus according to Josephus (Antiq., 19.6.2), and also

8:10 and to whomsoever the Lord shall show a sign, his wife shall she be."

8:11 And the heralds went out through all the circuit of Judæa, and the trumpet of the Lord sounded[41], and all ran.

CHAPTER IX

9:1 And Joseph, throwing away his axe, went out to meet them;

9:2 and when they had assembled, they went away to the high priest, taking with them their rods.

9:3 And he, taking the rods of all of them, entered into the temple, and prayed;

9:4 and having ended his prayer, he took the rods and came out, and gave them to them: but there was no sign in them, and Joseph took his rod last;

9:5 and, behold, a dove came out of the rod, and flew upon Joseph's head.

9:6 And the priest said to Joseph, "You have been chosen by lot[42] to take into your keeping the virgin of the Lord.

9:7 But Joseph refused, saying: "I have children[43], and I am an old man, and she is a young girl.

9:8 I am afraid lest I become a laughing-stock to the sons of Israel."

---

found in later Talmudic references (*Pesahim, 57a; Tosefta Menahot, 13:12*). Alternatively, this might be an allusion toe Zechariah, father of John the Baptist (Luke 1:67-79), although he does not act as high priest.

[41] This is a curious episode as traditionally the 'trumpets of the Lord' are not used to gather elders of Israel. While this could apply to either a 'shofar' or a 'hasosrah', neither are employed for such a convocation. The most common use was in the temple rituals during the Jewish New Year festival, or the new moon (Ps. 81:3), or a Jubilee Year (Lev. 25:9), or the start of a war (Josh. 6:4; Jud. 3:27, 7:16-20; 1 Sam. 8:3). It is far more likely that, if this convocation took place, it was associated with Rosh Hashanah, which was commonly known colloquially as Yom Teruah, the 'feast of the blast.'

[42] It seems that this casting of lots was more likely akin to the practice of 'urim and thummim', which was noted as being employed for the purposes of cleromancy (1 Sam. 14:41). Within the context of the High Priest this would appear to be consistent, as he appears to be the sole proprietor of this legitimization of divination.

[43] While these sons are mentioned in the synoptic gospels (Matt. 13:55), Epiphanius of Salamis grants the names of his daughters as well as Mary and Salome, both common names of the period (*Panarion, 78.8-9*). Epiphanius lays claim that these are Joseph's children from a previous marriage, which the author(s) of this text appears to agree with.

9:9 And the priest said to Joseph: "Fear the Lord your God, and remember what the Lord did to Dathan, and Abiram, and Korah[44];

9:10 how the earth opened, and they were swallowed up on account of their contradiction.

9:11 And now fear, O Joseph, lest the same things happen in your house."

9:12 And Joseph was afraid and took her into his keeping.

9:13 And Joseph said to Mary: "Behold, I have received you from the temple of the Lord; and now I leave you in my house[45], and go away to build my buildings, and I shall come to you.

9:14 The Lord will protect you.

CHAPTER X

10:1 And there was a council of the priests, saying: "Let us make a veil for the temple of the Lord."[46]

10:2 And the priest said: "Call to me the undefiled virgins of the family of David.[47]"

10:3 And the officers went away, and sought, and found seven virgins[48].

---

[44] See Num. 16:31-33

[45] The point of origin for Joseph and his immediate family is unclear. While he is associated with Bethlehem, there is significantly less of an ecclesiastical tradition regarding the early life of Joseph. There are various potential candidates for the native home of Joseph, but none fully fit the limited information provided by tradition.

[46] This first sentence appears out of place, or that it is missing part of the narrative. Presumably, the veil of the temple (Ex. 26:31, 36:35; 2 Chr. 3:14) is manufactured by these women. Since Mary is allegedly a spinner she would have been among their ranks. References to the veil of the temple are rare, so there is no account to confirm nor deny the existence of this tradition.

[47] The references to the House of David is rare in antiquity. Josephus mentions various messianic figures, but no clear association is ever drawn by him. Why there are various chaste members of the House of David appears strange. The exact nature of their progeny is unclear, but they must have been partially prolific as the Roman Emperor Domitian order their execution (*Eusebius, Ecclesiastical History, 3.19-20*). Later Arab chroniclers certainly make note of a specific Davidic heir named Liunan ben Babbutan (*History of al-Tabari, IV.741*) as being a contemporary of Christ. This name, whatever its origins, appears to be a corruption of the transliteration of the name 'Hunan ben Rav Natan'.

[48] This motif of seven virgins is also found in the Infancy Gospel of Mary, where they are noted as having been educated together at the temple.

10:4 And the priest remembered the child Mary, that she was of the family of David[49], and undefiled before God.

10:5 And the officers went away and brought her.

10:6 And they brought them into the temple of the Lord.

10:7 And the priest said: "Choose for me by lot who shall spin the gold, and the white, and the fine linen, and the silk, and the blue, and the scarlet, and the true purple.[50]

10:8 And the true purple and the scarlet fell to the lot of Mary, and she took them, and went away to her house.

10:9 And at that time Zacharias was dumb, and Samuel was in his place until the time that Zacharias spoke.

10:10 And Mary took the scarlet and span it[51].

CHAPTER XI

11:1 And she took the pitcher and went out to fill it with water.

---

[49] The scarcity of references to the family of David makes for a difficult historical riddle. The Arab historian al-Makrizi makes a passing reference to the descendants of David leaving Judea during the Hashomean dynasty. The first such reference in rabbinical literature to a Davidic heir is 'Ahijah' the Babylonian (*Berakhot, 63a, b*) who sought civic autonomy from the Jerusalem Sanhedrin sometime in the early 2nd century. The exact nature of Mary's Davidic descent appears unclear in both Christian literature and Jewish polemics of this period. While it is not mentioned in the Gospel accounts it is mentioned within the 1st century (*Ignatius, Letter to the Ephesiains, XVIII; Justin Martyr, Dialogus cum Tryphone Judaeo*). Later, emphasis on her Davidic family was noted by Tertullian (*De Carni Christi, 20*), who sought to counter Docetic claims about Christ's humanity. Augustine appears to place no emphasis on Mary's genealogy, instead laying primacy with Joseph the Carpenter's Davidic descent (*De Consensu Evangelistarum, 2.1.2-4; Sermon 1.16-21*). Collectively, the Church Fathers levied the theory that Luke's genealogy relates to Joseph, and that Matthew's relates to Mary (*Clement, Stromata, 21; Victorinus of Pettau, In Apocalypsin, 4.7-10; Irenaeus, Adversus Haereses, 3.21.9*). However, this is not stated in the Gospel accounts, and is improbable given the genealogical expectations of the period. The inverse claim, that Luke's genealogy belongs to Mary has also been claimed, curiously by both Jewish (*Doctrina Jacobi, 1.42*) and Christian sources (*Andronicus Palealogos, Dialogus contra Iudaeos, 38; John of Damascus, De Fide Orthodoxa, 4.14; Andrew of Crete, Oration VI; Epiphanius the Monks, Sermo de vita sanctissimae deiparae*). Since Luke's genealogy does not employ the word 'son', this is possible, but the reasons for this strange utilization is unclear.

[50] See Ex. 25:4

[51] Both the anti-Christian polemist Celsus and the Talmud do relate the Mary was occupationally trained as a spinner. This is also a common motif in Medieval art, where Mary is commonly portrayed as holding the thread of life. This would not be an uncommon occupation for a Jewish woman in antiquity, but it would have been perceived as below the royal dignity of the aristocracy.

11:2 And, behold, a voice saying: "Hail, you who hast received grace; the Lord is with you; blessed are you among women!"[52]

11:3 And she looked round, on the right hand and on the left, to see whence this voice came.

11:4 And she went away, trembling, to her house, and put down the pitcher;

11:5 and taking the purple, she sat down on her seat, and drew it out.

11:6 And, behold, an angel of the Lord stood before her, saying: "Fear not, Mary; for you have found grace before the Lord of all, and you shall conceive, according to His word."

11:7 And she hearing, reasoned with herself, saying: "Shall I conceive by the Lord, the living God?

11:8 And shall I bring forth as every woman brings forth?"

11:9 And the angel of the Lord said: "Not so, Mary; for the power of the Lord shall overshadow you: wherefore also that holy thing which shall be born of you shall be called the Son of the Most High.

11:10 And you shall call His name Jesus, for He shall save His people from their sins."

11:11 And Mary said: "Behold, the servant of the Lord before His face: let it be unto me according to your word."

---

[52] See Luke 1:28

CHAPTER XII

12:1   And she made the purple and the scarlet and took them to the priest.

12:2   And the priest blessed her, and said: "Mary, the Lord God has magnified your name, and you shall be blessed in all the generations of the earth.

12:3 And Mary, with great joy, went away to Elizabeth her kinswoman[53], and knocked at the door."

12:4 And when Elizabeth heard her, she threw away the scarlet, and ran to the door, and opened it; and seeing Mary, she blessed her, and said: "Whence is this to me, that the mother of my Lord should come to me?

12:5 For, behold, that which is in me leaped and blessed you[54]."

12:6 But Mary had forgotten the mysteries of which the archangel Gabriel had spoken, and gazed up into heaven, and said: "Who am I, O Lord, that all the generations of the earth should bless me?[55]"

12:7 And she remained three months with Elizabeth;

12:8 and day by day she grew bigger.

12:9 And Mary being afraid, went away to her own house, and hid herself from the sons of Israel.

12:10 And she was sixteen years old[56] when these mysteries happened.

---

[53] See Luke 1:39-40, the exact nature of this relationship is unspecified in the Gospels. The Byzantine hagiographers claim that Mary's mother Anne was the sister of Sobe/Sofia, who was mother to Elizabeth. This is also the relationship specified by both the Ethiopian and Coptic Synaxarium.

[54] See Luke 1:34, 44

[55] See Luke 1:48

56 While this passage largely recounts the familiar account from Luke's gospel, it does grant this added detail to the narrative. The exact age of Mary appears to vary in each account. In the earliest of these she was thirteen years old at the conception of Christ (*Agapius of Hieropolis, Universal History, I*).

CHAPTER XIII

13:1 And she was in her sixth month; and, behold, Joseph came back from his building[57], and, entering into his house, he discovered that she was big with child.

13:2 And he smote his face, and threw himself on the ground upon the sackcloth, and wept bitterly, saying: "With what face shall I look upon the Lord my God?

13:3 And what prayer shall I make about this maiden?

13:4 Because I received her a virgin out of the temple of the Lord, and I have not watched over her.

13:5 Who is it that has hunted me down?

13:6 Who has done this evil thing in my house, and defiled the virgin?

13:7 Has not the history of Adam been repeated in me?

13:8 For just as Adam was in the hour of his singing praise, and the serpent came, and found Eve alone, and completely deceived her, so it has happened to me also."

13:9 And Joseph stood up from the sackcloth, and called Mary, and said to her: "O you who hast been cared for by God, why have you done this and forgotten the Lord your God?

13:10 Why have you brought low your soul, you that wast brought up in the holy of holies, and that received food from the hand of an angel?"

13:11 And she wept bitterly, saying: "I am innocent, and have known no man."

13:12 And Joseph said to her: "Whence then is that which is in your womb?"

13:13 And she said: "As the Lord my God lives, I do not know whence it is to me."

---

[57] Some texts indicate that he was 'building houses abroad', which is a curious account of Joseph's life. Since this was during the reign of Herod the Great, 'abroad' could mean the Decapolis Confederation to the East, the Roman Province of Coele-Syria to the North, or the Kingdom of Nabatea to the South. However, given the extensive Coptic tradition of Christ's family in Egypt, temporary residence in Roman Egypt seems the most likely option. Christ's ties to Egypt appear among the anti-Christian polemists of the period (*Origen, Against Celsus, 1.28*) as well in various Coptic hagiography of the 4th and 5th centuries.

CHAPTER XIV

14:1 And Joseph was greatly afraid, and retired from her, and considered what he should do in regard to her[58].

14:2 And Joseph said: "If I conceal her sin, I find myself fighting against the law of the Lord;

14:3 and if I expose her to the sons of Israel, I am afraid lest that which is in her be from an angel, and I shall be found giving up innocent blood to the doom of death.

14:4 What then shall I do with her?

14:5 I will put her away from me secretly."

14:6 And night came upon him; and, behold, an angel of the Lord appears to him in a dream, saying: "Be not afraid for this maiden, for that which is in her is of the Holy Spirit;

14:7 and she will bring forth a Son, and you shall call His name 'Jesus', for He will save His people from their sins."[59]

14:8 And Joseph arose from sleep, and glorified the God of Israel, who had given him this grace; and he kept her.

CHAPTER XV

15:1 And Annas the scribe[60] came to him and said: "Why have you not appeared in our assembly?"[61]

---

[58] See Matt. 1:19

[59] See Matt. 1:20

[60] While 'Annas' is a derivative of the formal name 'Hananiah', it is tempting to associate this reference to the Jewish High Priest, Annas ben Seth, made famous as the founder of a political dynasty during the post Herodian period (*Josephus, Antiq. 20.9.1*). However, there is nothing that would specify that they are one in the same person.

[61] Presumably this is in reference to the Sanhedrin in Jerusalem, which was intended to be composed of the senior families of Judea. However, this appears precarious as the royal administration of Herod the Great appeared concerned with potential rival claimants. Having an identified Davidic heir as a member of this governing body would pose an intolerable threat and would be unlikely to be tolerated under that regime. Unfortunately, rabbinical accounts only preserve later interactions between the Sanhedrin and Davidic Princes, (*Horayat, 13b; Sanhedrin, 19a; Berakhot, 63a, b; Kilahim, 32b*), all of which appear to have a latent hostility attached to them. Inevitably this should not be surprising politically, as the legitimate source of author was largely vested in the High Priest in the post-exilic epoch, and with the demise of that office, conflict must have arisen out of this power vacuum.

15:2   And Joseph said to him: "Because I was weary from my journey and rested the first day."

15:3   And he turned, and saw that Mary was with child.

15:4   And he ran away to the priest, and said to him: "Joseph, whom you vouched for, has committed a grievous crime."

15:5   And the priest said: "How so?"

15:6   And he said: "He has defiled the virgin whom he received out of the temple of the Lord, and has married her by stealth, and has not revealed it to the sons of Israel."

15:7   And the priest answering, said: "Has Joseph done this?"

15:8   Then said Annas the scribe: "Send officers, and you will find the virgin with child."

15:9   And the officers went away and found it as he had said;

15:10   and they brought her along with Joseph to the tribunal.

15:11   And the priest said: "Mary, why have you done this? And why have you brought your soul low, and forgotten the Lord your God?

15:12   You that wast reared in the holy of holies, and that received food from the hand of an angel, and heard the hymns, and danced before Him, why have you done this?"[62]

15:13   And she wept bitterly, saying: "As the Lord my God lives, I am pure before Him, and know not a man."

15:14   And the priest said to Joseph: "Why have you done this?"

15:15   And Joseph said: "As the Lord lives, I am pure concerning her."

15:16   Then said the priest: "Bear not false witness, but speak the truth.

15:17   You have married her by stealth, and hast not revealed it to the sons of Israel, and hast not bowed your head under the strong hand, that your seed might be blessed."

15:18   And Joseph was silent.

---

[62] The nature of this offense appears poorly specified, as the vows of virginity were not accepted as part of Jewish law.

CHAPTER XVI

16:1   And the priest said: "Give up the virgin whom you received out of the temple of the Lord."

16:2   And Joseph burst into tears.

16:3   And the priest said: "I will give you to drink of the water of the ordeal of the Lord, and He shall make manifest your sins in your eyes.[63]"

16:4   And the priest took the water, and gave Joseph to drink and sent him away to the hill-country;

16:5   and he returned unhurt.

16:6   And he gave to Mary also to drink and sent her away to the hill-country;

16:7   and she returned unhurt.

16:8   And all the people wondered that sin did not appear in them.

16:9   And the priest said: "If the Lord God has not made manifest your sins, neither do I judge you."

16:10 And he sent them away.

16:11 And Joseph took Mary, and went away to his own house, rejoicing and glorifying the God of Israel.

CHAPTER XVII

17:1   And there was an order from the Emperor Augustus, that all in Bethlehem of Judæa should be enrolled.[64]

17:2   And Joseph said: "I shall enroll my sons[65], but what shall I do with this maiden?

---

[63] This is an obscure observance in Jewish legal practice of the period (Num. 5:18)

[64] See Luke 2:1, albeit a slight variation as the account in Luke grants that it was a census under the Prefect of Syria. The exact meaning of this census has never been fully understood, as no such means of collecting taxes was ever evoked in the Roman Empire.

[65] This account grants that Joseph the Carpenter's sons were from a previous marriage, which the Greek Fathers appear to assume in their writings. (*Epiphanius, Panarion, 28.7.6, 29.3.9; Origen, Commentary on Matthew, 10:17; History of Joseph the Carpenter, II*). St. Jerome grants her a name in his own writing, calling Esha or Melcha, but refuting the claim that of the Greek Fathers, and claiming that these were cousins (*Commentary on Matthew i*). Unlike Epiphanius Jerome does not grant us any point of citation for this claim. Some Latin Fathers appear to disagree with Jerome, citing the lack of a legal custodian to Mary with the death of Christ

17:3 How shall I enroll her? As my wife? I am ashamed.

17:4 As my daughter then? But all the sons of Israel know that she is not my daughter.

17:5 The day of the Lord shall itself bring it to pass as the Lord will."

17:6 And he saddled the ass[66] and set her upon it;

17:7 and his son[67] led it, and Joseph followed[68].

17:8 And when they had come within three miles, Joseph turned and saw her sorrowful;

17:9 and he said to himself: Likely that which is in her distresses her.

17:10 And again, Joseph turned and saw her laughing. And he said to her: "Mary, how is it that I see in your face at one time laughter, at another sorrow?"

17:11 And Mary said to Joseph: "Because I see two peoples with my eyes;

17:12 the one weeping and lamenting, and the other rejoicing and exulting."

17:13 And they came into the middle of the road, and Mary said to him: "Take me down from off the ass, for that which is in me presses to come forth."

17:14 And he took her down from off the ass, and said to her: "Whither shall I lead you, and cover your disgrace?"[69]

17:15 For the place is desert.

(*Hilary of Poitiers, Commentary on Matthew 1:1*) and the ambiguity of the term brothers (*Ambrose, De Instiutiane Virginis, 2.160*).

[66] See Zech. 9:9

[67] This would have been a duty assigned to a son that had reached 'adulthood' and was therefore over the age of thirteen. Assuming that this duty fell to his eldest son, James/Jacob, he would have been born around the year 20 BC and was only slightly younger than that of his step-mother, Mary. Josephus claims that he was stoned to death by the High Priest Ananus ben Ananus, around the year 63 BC. This would give us the age of his death at around 83 years of age. (*Antiq., 20.9*) However, some texts name the son as 'Simon', which would place James as being over 83 years of age at the time of his death.

[68] Some manuscripts have "And his son Samuel led it, and James and Simon followed." While James and Simon are known personalities, Samuel is both unknown and the use of "his son" can only be indicative of another editorial removal. Since this only appears in the minority of manuscripts this omission must have taken place in antiquity.

[69] Curiously, while this account follows the Lucan account closely it does not yet mention a place called 'Nazareth' relating to the life of Mary of Joseph. The reference that they are passing over desert here is also strange given the nature of the synoptic infancy narratives. There are no significant stretches of wilderness between Galilee and Judea. Territory that is uninhabitable generally lies to east of the river Jordan, in Idumea south of Jerusalem, and the Negev region west of Judea.

CHAPTER XVIII

18:1   And he found a cave[70] there, and led her into it;

18:2   and leaving his two sons beside her, he went out to seek a midwife in the district of Bethlehem.

18:3   And I, Joseph,[71] was walking and was not walking;

18:4   and I looked up into the sky and saw the sky astonished;

18:5   and I looked up to the pole of the heavens, and saw it standing, and the birds of the air keeping still.

18:6   And I looked down upon the earth, and saw a trough lying, and work people reclining, and their hands were in the trough.

18:7   And those that were eating did not eat, and those that were rising did not carry it up, and those that were conveying anything to their mouths did not convey it;

18:8   but the faces of all were looking upwards.

18:9   And I saw the sheep walking, and the sheep stood still;

18:10   and the shepherd raised his hand to strike them, and his hand remained up.

18:11   And I looked upon the current of the river, and I saw the mouths of the kids resting on the water and not drinking, and all things in a moment were driven from their course.

---

[70] The hamlet of Bethlehem used to be overshadowed by a grove of Thammuz/Adonis;. St. Jerome makes note in his Letter to Paulinus that in the cave where Christ formerly wailed as an infant, they used to mourn for the beloved of Venus. St. Jerome also references this cave in his Letter to Sabinianus, the "cave in which the Son of God was born;" "that venerable cave," et cetera., "within the door of what was once the Lord's manger, now the altar." Justin Marytr appears to also allude to it (*Dialgoue with Trypho, 78*).

[71] The narrative has a sudden shift in voice and diction that appears to be unrelated to all previous sections. This appears to be a later textual introjection to give the document added authority within the developing Christian community. Also, unlike previous sections, it does not appear to have any association with Jewish liturgical ritual.

CHAPTER XIX

19:1	And I saw a woman coming down from the hill-country, and she said to me: "O man, whither are you going?"
19:2	And I said: "I am seeking a Hebrew midwife." And she answered and said to me: "Are you of Israel?"
19:3	And I said to her: "Yes."
19:4	And she said: "And who is it that is bringing forth in the cave?"
19:5	And I said: "A woman betrothed to me."

19:6   And she said to me: "Is she not your wife?"

19:7   And I said to her: "It is Mary that was reared in the temple of the Lord, and I obtained her by lot as my wife. And yet she is not my wife but has conceived of the Holy Spirit."

19:8   And the midwife said to him: "Is this true?"

19:9   And Joseph[72] said to her: "Come and see."[73]

19:10 And the midwife went away with him.

19:11 And they stood in the place of the cave, and behold a luminous cloud overshadowed the cave.

19:12 And the midwife said: "My soul has been magnified this day, because my eyes have seen strange things — because salvation has been brought forth to Israel."

19:13 And immediately the cloud disappeared out of the cave, and a great light shone in the cave, so that the eyes could not bear it.

19:14 And in a little that light gradually decreased, until the infant appeared, and went and took the breast from His mother Mary.

19:15 And the midwife cried out and said: "This is a great day to me, because I have seen this strange sight."

19:16 And the midwife went forth out of the cave, and Salome[74] met her.

19:17 And she said to her: "Salome, Salome, I have a strange sight to relate to you: a virgin has brought forth — a thing which her nature admits not of."

19:18 Then said Salome: "As the Lord my God lives, unless I thrust in my finger, and search the parts, I will not believe that a virgin has brought forth."[75]

CHAPTER XX

20:1   And the midwife went in and said to Mary: "Show yourself; for no small controversy has arisen about you."

---

[72] Here the text switches back from the first person to the third person.

[73] This response appears pregnant with religious meaning. It is used elsewhere regarding the piety of those who reside in Nazareth (John 1:46)

[74] The identity of this Salome appears as a matter of dispute. Because of the popularity of the name, she is likely a different individual from the disciple of Christ during his ministry (Mark 15:40).

[75] See parallel John 21:25

20:2 And Salome put in her finger, and cried out, and said: "Woe is me for mine iniquity and mine unbelief, because I have tempted the living God;

20:3 and, behold, my hand is dropping off as if burned with fire."

20:4 And she bent her knees before the Lord, saying: "O God of my fathers, remember that I am the seed of Abraham, and Isaac, and Jacob;

20:5 do not make a show of me to the sons of Israel, but restore me to the poor;

20:6 for You know, O Lord, that in Your name I have performed my services, and that I have received my reward at Your hand."

20:7 And, behold, an angel of the Lord stood by her, saying to her: "Salome, Salome, the Lord has heard you.

20:8 Put your hand to the infant, and carry it, and you will have safety and joy."

20:9 And Salome went and carried it, saying: "I will worship Him, because a great King has been born to Israel."

20:10 And, behold, Salome was immediately cured, and she went forth out of the cave justified.

20:11 And behold a voice saying: "Salome, Salome, tell not the strange things you have seen, until the child has come into Jerusalem."

CHAPTER XXI

21:1   And, behold, Joseph was ready to go into Judæa. And there was a great commotion in Bethlehem of Judæa, for Magi came, saying: "Where is he that is born king of the Jews?

21:2   For we have seen his star in the east and have come to worship him."

21:3   And when Herod heard, he was much disturbed, and sent officers to the Magi.

21:4 And he sent for the priests, and examined them, saying: "How is it written about the Christ?

21:5 Where is He to be born?"

21:6 And they said: "In Bethlehem of Judæa, for so it is written[76]."

21:7 And he sent them away.

21:8 And he examined the Magi, saying to them: "What sign have you seen in reference to the king that has been born?"

21:9 And the Magi said: "We have seen a star of great size shining among these stars, and obscuring their light, so that the stars did not appear;

21:10 and we thus knew that a king has been born to Israel, and we have come to worship him."

21:11 And Herod said: "Go and seek him; and if you find him, let me know, in order that I also may go and worship him."

21:12 And the Magi went out.

21:13 And, behold, the star which they had seen in the east went before them until they came to the cave[77], and it stood over the top of the cave.

21:14 And the Magi saw the infant with His mother Mary;

21:15 and they brought forth from their bag gold, and frankincense, and myrrh.

21:16 And having been warned by the angel not to go into Judæa, they went into their own country by another road.

CHAPTER XXII

22:1 And when Herod knew that he had been mocked by the Magi, in a rage he sent murderers, saying to them: "Slay the children from two years old and under."

22:2 And Mary, having heard that the children were being killed, was afraid, and took the infant and swaddled Him[78], and put Him into an ox-stall[79].

---

[76] Some manuscripts include the quote from Micah 5:2

[77] This account stands in conflict with that of Matthew's Gospel which makes no reference to a cave, but to a house (Matt. 2:11). Ergo, the author(s) must have had a source independent of the synoptic Gospel accounts. Later Christian writers appear to be familiar wit this cave, as they make note of it as being outside of Bethlehem proper (*Justin Martyr, Dialogue with Trypho, 78; Origen, Against Celsus, 1.51*)

22:3 And Elizabeth, having heard that they were searching for John, took him and went up into the hill-country, and kept looking where to conceal him.

22:4 And there was no place of concealment.

22:5 And Elizabeth, groaning with a loud voice, says: "O mountain of God, receive mother and child."

22:6 And immediately the mountain was cleft and received her."[80]

22:7 And a light shone about them, for an angel of the Lord was with them, watching over them.

CHAPTER XXIII

23:1 And Herod searched for John, and sent officers to Zacharias, saying: "Where have you hid your son?"

23:2 And he, answering, said to them: "I am the servant of God in holy things, and I sit constantly in the temple of the Lord: I do not know where my son is."

23:3 And the officers went away and reported all these things to Herod.

23:4 And Herod was enraged, and said: "His son is destined to be king over Israel.[81]"

23:5 And he sent to him again, saying: "Tell the truth; where is your son?

---

[78] While this has parallels to the Lucan narrative of the nativity (Luke 2:7), it is chronological different here.

[79] This is a strange account, as the flight into Egypt is not mentioned in this text. The narrative simply ignores Christ's place in Herod's plot and instead places emphasis on the threat to John the Baptist's life. Moreover, the narrative comes to no formal conclusion at this point, but simply stops dead. Christ's Egyptian nativity appears to be attested to in both Jewish (*Babylonian Sabbat, 104b, Jerusalem Sabbat, 12:4; Quddushin, 49b; Huldricus, Historia Jeshuae Nazareni, 20,24*). Coptic and Assyrian account grant added details to the occurrence, but never ignore this part of the narrative altogether.

[80] This story does not appear in the synoptic accounts. It does infer that Elizabeth was a resident of Bethlehem. Josephus, while identifying John the Baptist as a historical personality, makes no identification of him with the relatively small city of Bethlehem. A similar miraculous occurrence is found in the 'Acts of Paul and Thecla'.

[81] Why Herod would have been threatened by John the Baptist is uncertain, as John was not of Davidic descent. His priestly lineage might be a potential threat if he was perceived as being the rightful claimant to the High Priest. However, neither the synoptic Gospels nor Josephus make any allusion to this occurrence.

23:6 For you know that your life is in my hand." And Zacharias said: "I am God's martyr, if you shed my blood;

23:7 for the Lord will receive my spirit, because you shed innocent blood at the vestibule of the temple of the Lord."

23:8 And Zacharias was murdered about daybreak[82].

23:9 And the sons of Israel did not know that he had been murdered.

[82] There appears to be a certain parallel in rabbinical literature regarding the death of Zachariah the priest (*Taanith, 69; Sanhedrin, 96*), attesting to his importance, but not necessarily his identity. While this account comes down through rabbinical source, Josephus makes no such reference.

CHAPTER XXIV

24:1   But at the hour of the salutation the priests went away, and Zacharias did not come forth to meet them with a blessing, according to his custom.

24:2   And the priests stood waiting for Zacharias to salute him at the prayer, and to glorify the Most High.

24:3   And he still delaying, they were all afraid.

24:4   But one of them ventured to go in, and he saw clotted blood beside the altar;

24:5   and he heard a voice saying: "Zacharias has been murdered, and his blood shall not be wiped up until his avenger come."

24:6   And hearing this saying, he was afraid, and went out and told it to the priests.

24:7   And they ventured in and saw what had happened;

24:8   and the fretwork of the temple made a wailing noise, and they rent their clothes from the top even to the bottom.

24:9   And they found not his body, but they found his blood turned into stone.

24:10   And they were afraid and went out and reported to the people that Zacharias had been murdered.

24:11   And all the tribes of the people heard, and mourned, and lamented for him three days and three nights.

24:12   And after the three days, the priests consulted as to whom they should put in his place;

24:13   and the lot fell upon Simeon[83].

24:14   For it was he who had been warned by the Holy Spirit that he should not see death until he should see the Christ in the flesh.

24:15   And I, James[84], that wrote this history in Jerusalem, a commotion having arisen when Herod died, withdrew myself to the wilderness until the commotion in Jerusalem ceased,

---

[83] While Zechariah was not listed among the High Priests of Israel, the identity of this Simeon is broad. He could be the Nasi of the Sanhedrin, Simeon ben Hillel, which would explain the absence of information regarding Zechariah. However, Simeon ben Hillel is relatively unknown in any historical record. The author was more likely than not drawing upon Luke's narrative, as the infant Christ meets with an unknown temple resident named Simeon (Luke 2;25).

[84] This too appears to a later addition to grant the text legitimacy. While it appears in the oldest intact manuscripts of this Gospel, James was not regarded as having abided in Jerusalem until after the execution of Christ some three decades later.

glorifying the Lord God, who had given me the gift and the wisdom to write this history.

24:16   And grace shall be with them that fear our Lord Jesus Christ, to whom be glory to ages of ages. Amen.

THE PROTOEVANGELIUM OF JAMES

Byzantine Greek Text
Codex C (Paris 1454, 10th CE)

1

1 Ἐν ταῖς ἱστορίαις τῶν δώδεκα φυλῶν τοῦ Ἰσραὴλ ἦν Ἰωακεὶμ πλούσιος σφόδρα, καὶ προσέφερε κυρίῳ τὰ δῶρα αὐτοῦ διπλᾶ λέγων ἐν ἑαυτῷ: Ἔσται τὸ τῆς περισσείας μου ἅπαντι τῷ λαῷ καὶ τὸ τῆς ἀφέσεως κυρίῳ τῷ θεῷ εἰς ἱλασμὸν ἐμοί. 2 ἐνήγγισεν δὲ ἡ ἡμέρα κυρίου ἡ μεγάλη καὶ προσέφερον οἱ υἱοὶ Ἰσραὴλ τὰ δῶρα αὐτῶν, καὶ ἔστη κατενώπιον αὐτοῦ καὶ Ρουβὴλ λέγων: οὐκ ἔξεστίν σοι πρώτῳ προσενεγκεῖν τὰ δῶρά σου, καθότι σπέρμα οὐκ ἐποίησας ἐν τῷ Ἰσραήλ. 3 καὶ ἐλυπήθη Ἰωακεὶμ καὶ ἀπίει εἰς τὸν οἶκον αὐτοῦ, καὶ ἐλθὼν εἰς τὴν δωδεκάφυλον τοῦ λαοῦ λέγει: ὄψομαι, εἰ ἐγὼ μόνος οὐκ ἐποίησα σπέρμα ἐν τῷ Ἰσραήλ. ἠρεύνησε δὲ καὶ εὗρε πάντας τοὺς δικαίους, ὅτι σπέρμα ἀνέστησαν ἐν τῷ Ἰσραήλ, καὶ ἐμνήσθη τοῦ πατριάρχου Ἀβραάμ, ὅτι ἐν ταῖς ἐσχάταις αὐτοῦ ἡμέραις ἔδωκεν αὐτῷ ὁ θεὸς υἱὸν Ἰσαάκ. 4 καὶ ἐλυπεῖτο Ἰωακεὶμ σφόδρα καὶ οὐκ ἐφάνη τῇ γυναικὶ αὐτοῦ, ἀλλὰ ἔδωκεν ἑαυτὸν εἰς τὴν ἔρημον, καὶ ἔπηξε τὴν σκηνὴν αὐτοῦ ἐκεῖ καὶ ἐνήστευσεν ἡμέρας τεσσεράκοντα καὶ νύκτας τεσσεράκοντα λέγων ἐν ἑαυτῷ: οὐ καταβήσομαι οὔτε ἐπὶ βρωτὸν οὔτε ἐπὶ ποτόν, ἕως ἐπισκέψηταί με κύριος ὁ θεός μου, καὶ ἔσται μοι ἡ εὐχὴ βρόματα καὶ πόματα.

2

1 Ἡ δὲ γυνὴ δὲ αὐτοῦ Ἄννα δύο θρήνους ἐθρήνει καὶ δύο κοπετοὺς ἐκόπτετο λέγουσα: κόψομαι τὴν χηρίαν μου καὶ κόψομαι τὴν ἀτεκνίαν μου. 2 ἤγγισε δὲ ἡ ἡμέρα κυρίου ἡ μεγάλη καὶ εἶπεν Ἰουδὴθ ἡ παιδίσκη αὐτῆς πρὸς αὐτήν: ἕως πότε ταπεινοῖς τὴν ψυχήν σου; ἰδοὺ γὰρ ἤγγισεν ἡ ἡμέρα κυρίου ἡ μεγάλη καὶ οὐκ ἔξεστί σοι πενθεῖν. ἀλλὰ λάβε τοῦτο τὸ κεφαλοδέσμιον, ὃ ἔδωκέν μοι ἡ κυρία τοῦ ἔργου, καὶ οὐκ ἔξεστί μοι ἀναδήσασθαι αὐτό, καθότι παιδίσκη σού εἰμι καὶ χαρακτῆρα ἔχει βασιλικόν. 3 καὶ εἶπεν Ἄννα: ἀπόστηθι ἀπ' ἐμοῦ: καὶ ταῦτα οὐκ ἐποίησα, καὶ κύριος ὁ θεὸς ἐταπείνωσέν με σφόδρα. μήπως

πανοῦργος ἔδωκέν σοι τοῦτο καὶ ἦλθες κοινωνῆσαί με τῇ ἁμαρτίᾳ σου; εἶπεν δὲ αὐτῇ Ἰουδὴθ ἡ παιδίσκη αὐτῆς: τί ἀράσωμαί σοι, καθότι οὐκ ἤκουσας τῆς φωνῆς μου; ἀπέκλεισεν κύριος ὁ θεὸς τὴν μήτραν σου τοῦ μὴ δοῦναί σοι καρπὸν ἐν τῷ Ἰσραήλ. 4 καὶ ἐλυπήθη Ἄννα σφόδρα καὶ περιείλετο τὰ ἱμάτια αὐτῆς τὰ πενθικὰ καὶ ἐσμήξατο τὴν κεφαλὴν αὐτῆς καὶ ἐνεδύσατο τὰ ἱμάτια αὐτῆς τὰ νυμφικὰ καὶ περὶ ὥραν ἐννάτην κατέβη εἰς τὸν παράδεισον αὐτῆς (τοῦ περιπατῆσαι). καὶ εἶδεν δάφνην καὶ ἐκάθισεν ὑποκάτω αὐτῆς καὶ ἐλιτάνευσε τῷ δεσπότῃ λέγουσα: ὁ θεὸς τῶν πατέρων μου, εὐλόγησόν με καὶ ἐπάκουσον τῆς δεήσεός μου, καθὼς ἐπήκουσας καὶ εὐλόγησας τὴν μητέραν Σάραν καὶ ἔδωκας αὐτῇ υἱὸν τὸν Ἰσαάκ.

3

1 Καὶ ἀτενίσασα Ἄννα εἰς οὐρανὸν εἶδεν καλιὰν στρουθίων ἐν τῇ δάφνῃ καὶ εὐθέως ἐποίησε θρῆνον ἐν ἑαυτῇ λέγουσα: οἴμοι, τίς με ἐγέννησεν, ποία δὲ μήτρα ἐξέφυσέν με, ὅτι κατάρα ἐγεννήθην ἐνώπιον τῶν υἱῶν Ἰσραὴλ καὶ ὠνειδίσθην καὶ ἐξεμυκτηρίσθην ἐκβληθεῖσα ἐκ ναοῦ κυρίου τοῦ θεοῦ μου; 2 οἴμοι, τίνι ὁμοιώθην ἐγώ; οὐχ ὁμοιώθην ἐγὼ τοῖς πετεινοῖς τοῦ οὐρανοῦ, ὅτι καὶ τὰ πετεινὰ γόνιμά εἰσιν ἐνώπιόν σου, κύριε. οἴμοι, τίνι ὁμοιώθην ἐγώ; οὐχ ὁμοιώθην ἐγὼ τοῖς ἀλόγοις ζώοις, καὶ τὰ ἄλογα ζῶα γόνιμά εἰσιν ἐνώπιόν σου, κύριε. 3 οἴμοι, τίνι ὁμοιώθην ἐγώ; οὐχ ὁμοιώθην ἐγὼ τοῖς ὕδασι τούτοις, ὅτι καὶ τὰ ὕδατα γόνιμά εἰσιν ἐνώπιόν σου, κύριε. οἴμοι, τίνι ὁμοιώθην ἐγώ; οὐχ ὁμοιώθην ἐγὼ τῇ γῇ, ὅτι καὶ ἡ γῆ προφέρει τοὺς καρποὺς αὐτῆς κατὰ καιρὸν καί σε εὐλογεῖ, κύριε.

4

1 Καὶ ἰδοὺ ἄγγελος κυρίου ἐπέστη λέγων: Ἄννα, Ἄννα, εἰσήκουσε κύριος ὁ θεὸς τῆς δεήσεός σου, καὶ λήψῃ καὶ λαληθήσεται τὸ σπέρμα σου ἐν ὅλῃ τῇ οἰκουμένῃ. εἶπεν δὲ Ἄννα: ζῇ κύριος ὁ θεός μου: ἐὰν γεννήσω εἴτε ἄρρεν εἴτε θῆλυ, προσάξω αὐτὸ δῶρον κυρίῳ τῷ θεῷ μου καὶ ἔσται λειτουργοῦν αὐτῷ πάσας ἡμέρας τῆς ζωῆς αὐτοῦ. 2 καὶ ἰδοὺ ἦλθοσαν ἄγγελοι δύο λέγοντες αὐτῇ: ἰδοὺ Ἰωακεὶμ ὁ ἀνήρ σου ἔρχεται μετὰ τῶν ποιμνίων αὐτοῦ. ἄγγελος γὰρ κυρίου κατέβη πρὸς

αὐτὸν λέγων· Ἰωακείμ, Ἰωακείμ, εἰσήκουσε κύριος ὁ θεὸς τῆς δεήσεός σου. κατάβηθι ἐντεῦθεν. ἰδοὺ Ἄννα ἡ γυνή σου ἐν γαστρὶ λήψεται (εἴληφεν). 3 καὶ εὐθέως κατέβη Ἰωακεὶμ καὶ ἐκάλεσεν τοὺς ποιμένας αὐτοῦ λέγων· φέρετέ μοι ὧδε δώδεκα ἀμνάδας ἀσπίλους καὶ ἀμόμους εἰς θυσίαν κυρίῳ τῷ θεῷ μου, καὶ φέρετέ μοι δώδεκα μόσχους ἀσπίλους καὶ ἔσονται τοῖς ἱερεῦσι καὶ τῇ γερουσίᾳ, καὶ φέρετέ μοι ἑκατὸν χιμάρους καὶ ἔσονται αἱ ἑκατὸν χίμαροι παντὶ τῷ λαῷ. 4 καὶ ἰδοὺ ἥκει Ἰωακεὶμ μετὰ τῶν ποιμνίων αὐτοῦ. καὶ ἔστη Ἄννα πρὸς τῇ πύλῃ τοῦ οἴκου αὐτῆς καὶ εἶδεν τὸν Ἰωακεὶμ ἐρχόμενον μετὰ τῶν ποιμνίων αὐτοῦ. καὶ ἔδραμεν Ἄννα καὶ ἐκρεμάσθη ἐπὶ τὸν τράχηλον αὐτοῦ λέγουσα· νῦν οἶδα, ὅτι κύριος ὁ θεὸς εὐλόγησέ με σφόδρα· ἰδοὺ γὰρ ἡ χήρα οὐκέτι χήρα καὶ ἡ ἄτεκνος ἰδοὺ ἐν γαστρὶ λήψομαι εἴληφα . καὶ ἀνεπαύσατο Ἰωακεὶμ τὴν πρώτην ἡμέραν εἰς τὸν οἶκον αὐτοῦ.

5

1 Τῇ δὲ ἐπαύριον προσέφερε τὰ δῶρα αὐτοῦ λέγων ἐν ἑαυτῷ· ἐὰν κύριος ὁ θεὸς ἱλασθῇ μοι, τὸ πέταλον τοῦ ἱερέως φανερὼν μοι ποιήσει. καὶ προσέφερεν τὰ δῶρα αὐτοῦ Ἰωακεὶμ καὶ προσεῖχε τῷ πετάλῳ τοῦ ἱερέως, ὡς ἐπέβη ἐπὶ τὸ θυσιαστήριον κυρίου, καὶ ἁμαρτία οὐχ εὑρέθη ἐν αὐτῷ. καὶ εἶπεν Ἰωακείμ· νῦν οἶδα, ὅτι κύριος ὁ θεὸς ἱλάσθη μοι καὶ ἀφεῖλέν μου πάντα τὰ ἁμαρτήματα. καὶ κατέβη ἐκ ναοῦ κυρίου δεδικαιωμένος καὶ ἀπῆλθεν εἰς τὸν οἶκον αὐτοῦ χαίρων καὶ δοξάζων τὸν θεόν. 2 ἐπληρώθησαν δὲ οἱ μῆνες αὐτῆς. ἐν δὲ τῷ ἐνάτῳ μηνὶ ἐγέννησεν Ἄννα καὶ εἶπεν τῇ μαίᾳ· τί ἐγέννησα; ἡ δὲ εἶπεν· θῆλυ. καὶ εἶπεν Ἄννα· ἐμεγάλυνεν ἡ ψυχή μου τὴν ἡμέραν ταύτην καὶ ἀνέκλινεν αὐτήν. πληρωθεισῶν δὲ τῶν ἡμερῶν ἀπεσμήξατο Ἄννα καὶ ἔδωκεν μασθὸν τῇ παιδί. ἐκάλεσεν δὲ τὸ ὄνομα αὐτῆς Μαριάμ.

6

1 Ἡμέρᾳ δὲ καὶ ἡμέρα ἐκραταιοῦτο ἡ παῖς. γενομένης δὲ αὐτῆς ἐξαμήνου ἔστησεν αὐτὴν ἡ μήτηρ αὐτῆς χαμαὶ τοῦ πειράσαι, εἰ ἵσταται· καὶ περιπατήσασα ἑπτὰ βήματα ἦλθεν εἰς τὸν κόλπον τῆς μητρὸς αὐτῆς, καὶ ἀνήρπασεν αὐτὴν ἡ μήτηρ αὐτῆς λέγουσα· ζῇ κύριος ὁ θεός μου· οὐ μὴ περιπατήσῃς ἐν τῇ γῇ

ταύτῃ, ἕως οὗ ἀπάξω σε ἐν τῷ ναῷ κυρίου. καὶ ἐποίησεν ἁγίασμα ἐν τῷ κοιτῶνι αὐτῆς καὶ πᾶν κοινὸν ἢ ἀκάθαρτον οὐκ εἴα διέρχεσθαι δι' αὐτῆς. καὶ ἐκάλεσε τὰς θυγατέρας τῶν Ἑβραίων τὰς ἀμιάντους, καὶ διεπλάνων αὐτήν. **2** ἐγένετο δὲ πρῶτος ἐνιαυτὸς τῇ παιδί, καὶ ἐποίησεν Ἰωακεὶμ δοχὴν μεγάλην καὶ ἐκάλεσεν τοὺς ἱερεῖς καὶ τοὺς γραμματεῖς καὶ τὴν γερουσίαν καὶ πάντα τὸν λαὸν Ἰσραήλ. καὶ προσήνεγκεν Ἰωακεὶμ τὴν παῖδα τοῖς ἱερεῦσι καὶ εὐλόγησαν αὐτὴν οἱ ἱερεῖς λέγοντες: ὁ θεὸς τῶν πατέρων ἡμῶν, εὐλόγησον τὴν παῖδα ταύτην καὶ δὸς αὐτῇ ὄνομα ὀνομαστὸν αἰώνιον ἐν πάσαις ταῖς γενεαῖς. καὶ εἶπεν ὁ λαός: γένοιτο, γένοιτο, ἀμήν. καὶ προσήνεγκεν Ἰωακεὶμ τὴν παῖδα τοῖς ἀρχιερεῦσι, καὶ εὐλόγησαν αὐτὴν λέγοντες: ὁ θεὸς τῶν ὑψωμάτων, ἐπίβλεψον ἐπὶ τὴν παῖδα ταύτην καὶ εὐλόγησον αὐτὴν ἐσχάτην εὐλογίαν, ἥτις διαδοχὴν οὐχ ἕξει. **3** καὶ ἀπήγαγον αὐτὴν ἐν τῷ ἁγιάσματι τοῦ κοιτῶνος αὐτῆς: καὶ λαβοῦσα Ἄννα ἔδωκε μασθὸν τῇ παιδὶ καὶ ᾖσεν ᾆσμα κυρίῳ τῷ θεῷ λέγουσα: ᾄσω ᾠδὴν κυρίῳ τῷ θεῷ μου, ὅτι ἐπεσκέψατό με καὶ ἀφεῖλεν ἀπ' ἐμοῦ τὸν ὀνειδισμὸν τῶν ἐχθρῶν μου καὶ ἔδωκέ μοι καρπὸν δικαιοσύνης μονοούσιον αὐτῷ καὶ πολυπλούσιον. τίς ἀναγγελεῖ τοῖς υἱοῖς Ῥουβίμ, ὅτι Ἄννα θηλάζει; καὶ ἀνέπαυσεν αὐτὴν ἡ μήτηρ αὐτῆς ἐν τῷ ἁγιάσματι τοῦ κοιτῶνος αὐτῆς καὶ ἐξῆλθε καὶ διηκόνει αὐτοῖς. τελεσθέντος δὲ τοῦ δείπνου κατέβησαν εὐφραινόμενοι καὶ ἐδόξασαν τὸν θεὸν Ἰσραήλ.

7

1 Τῇ δὲ παιδὶ προσετίθεντο οἱ μῆνες αὐτῆς. ἐγένετο δὲ διετὴς ἡ παῖς, καὶ εἶπεν Ἰωακείμ: ἀπάξωμεν αὐτὴν ἐν τῷ ναῷ κυρίου καὶ ἀποδῶμεν τὴν ἐπαγγελίαν, ἣν ἐπηγγειλάμεθα, μήπως ἀποστείλῃ κύριος ὁ θεὸς πρὸς ἡμᾶς καὶ γένηται ἀπρόσδεκτον τὸ δῶρον ἡμῶν. καὶ εἶπεν Ἄννα: ἀναμείνωμεν τὸ τρίτον ἔτος, ὅπως μὴ ζητήσῃ πατέρα ἢ μητέρα. καὶ εἶπεν Ἰωακείμ: ἀμήν, γένοιτο. **2** ἐγένετο δὲ τριετὴς ἡ παῖς, καὶ εἶπεν Ἰωακείμ: καλέσωμεν τὰς θυγατέρας τῶν Ἑβραίων τὰς ἀμιάντους, καὶ λαβέτωσαν ἀνὰ λαμπάδα, καὶ ἔστωσαν καιόμεναι, ἵνα μὴ ἐπιστραφῇ ἡ παῖς εἰς τὰ ὀπίσω καὶ αἰχμαλωτισθῇ ἡ καρδία αὐτῆς ἐκ ναοῦ κυρίου. καὶ ἐποίησαν οὕτως, ἕως οὗ ἀνέβησαν ἐν τῷ ναῷ κυρίου. καὶ ἐδέξατο αὐτὴν ὁ ἱερεὺς καὶ καταφιλήσας εὐλόγησε καὶ εἶπεν: ἐμεγάλυνε κύριος ὁ θεὸς τὸ ὄνομά σου ἐν πάσαις ταῖς γενεαῖς τῆς γῆς· (ἐπὶ σοὶ) ἐπ' ἐσχάτου τῶν ἡμερῶν φανερώσει κύριος ὁ θεὸς τὸ λύτρον τῶν υἱῶν Ἰσραήλ. **3** καὶ ἐκάθισεν αὐτὴν ἐπὶ τρίτου βαθμοῦ τοῦ θυσιαστηρίου, καὶ ἔβαλε κύριος ὁ θεὸς χάριν ἐπ' αὐτήν, καὶ κατεχόρευσε τοῖς ποσὶν αὐτοῖς, καὶ ἠγάπησεν αὐτὴν πᾶς οἶκος Ἰσραήλ.

8

1 κατέβησαν δὲ οἱ γονεῖς αὐτῆς θαυμάζοντες καὶ ἐπαινοῦντες τὸν θεόν, ὅτι οὐκ ἐπεστράφη ἡ παῖς εἰς τὰ ὀπίσω. ἦν δὲ Μαριὰμ ὡσεὶ περιστερὰ νεμομένη ἐν τῷ ναῷ κυρίου καὶ ἐλάμβανε τροφὴν ἐκ χειρὸς ἀγγέλου. **2** γενομένης δὲ αὐτῆς δωδεκαετοῦς συμβούλιον ἐγένετο τῶν ἱερέων λεγόντων· ἰδοὺ Μαριὰμ γέγονε δωδεκαέτης ἐν τῷ ναῷ κυρίου· τί οὖν ποιήσωμεν αὐτήν, μήπως (ἐπέλθῃ αὐτῇ τὰ γυναικῶν καὶ) μιάνῃ τὸ ἁγίασμα κυρίου. καὶ εἶπον τῷ ἀρχιερεῖ· σὺ ἕστηκας ἐπὶ τὸ θυσιαστήριον θεοῦ· εἴσελθε καὶ πρόσευξαι περὶ αὐτῆς, καὶ ὅ ἄν φανερώσῃ σοι κύριος ὁ θεός, τοῦτο ποιήσωμεν. **3** καὶ εἰσῆλθεν ὁ ἱερεὺς λαβὼν τὸν δωδεκακόδωνα (ἱεροπρεπὲς ἱμάτιον) εἰς τὰ ἅγια τῶν ἁγίων καὶ ηὔξατο περὶ αὐτῆς. καὶ ἰδοὺ ἄγγελος κυρίου ἐπέστη αὐτῷ λέγων· Ζαχαρία, Ζαχαρία, ἔξελθε καὶ ἐκκλησίασον τοὺς χηρεύοντας τοῦ λαοῦ, καὶ ἐνεγκάτωσαν ἀνὰ ῥάβδον, καὶ εἰς ὅν ἐὰν δείξῃ κύριος ὁ θεὸς σημεῖον, τούτου ἔσται γυνή. καὶ ἐξῆλθον οἱ κήρυκες καθ' ὅλης τῆς περιχώρου τῆς Ἰουδαίας, καὶ ἤχησεν ἡ σάλπιγξ κυρίου, καὶ ἔδραμον πάντες.

9

1 Ἰωσὴφ δὲ ῥίψας τὸ σκέπαρνον ἔδραμε καὶ αὐτὸς εἰς τὴν συναγωγήν, καὶ συναχθέντες ὁμοῦ ἀπῆλθαν πρὸς τὸν ἱερέα. ἔλαβε δὲ πάντων τὰς ῥάβδους ὁ ἱερεὺς καὶ εἰσῆλθεν εἰς τὸ ἱερὸν καὶ ηὔξατο. τελέσας δὲ τὴν εὐχὴν ἐξῆλθε καὶ ἐπέδωκεν ἑνὶ ἑκάστῳ τὴν ἑαυτοῦ ῥάβδον, καὶ σημεῖον οὐκ ἦν ἐν αὐτοῖς. τὴν δὲ ἐσχάτην ῥάβδον ἔλαβεν ὁ Ἰωσήφ, καὶ ἰδοὺ περιστερὰ ἐξῆλθεν ἐκ τῆς ῥάβδου καὶ ἐπετάσθη ἐπὶ τὴν κεφαλὴν Ἰωσήφ. καὶ εἶπεν αὐτῷ ὁ ἱερεύς· σὺ κεκλήρωσαι τὴν παρθένον κυρίου παραλαβεῖν. παράλαβε αὐτὴν εἰς τήρησιν σεαυτῷ. **2** ἀντεῖπε δὲ Ἰωσὴφ λέγων· υἱοὺς ἔχω καὶ πρεσβύτης εἰμί, αὕτη δὲ νεωτέρα. μήπως κατάγελως γένωμαι τοῖς υἱοῖς Ἰσραήλ; εἶπεν δὲ αὐτῷ ὁ ἱερεύς: Ἰωσήφ, φοβήθητι κύριον τὸν θεὸν καὶ ὅσα ἐποίησε Δαθὰμ καὶ Κορὲ καὶ Ἀβηρών, πῶς ἐδιχάσθη ἡ γῆ καὶ κατεποντίσθησαν ἅπαντες διὰ τὴν ἀντιλογίαν αὐτῶν. καὶ νῦν φοβήθητι, Ἰωσήφ, μήπως ἔσται ταῦτα ἐν τῷ οἴκῳ σου. 3 καὶ φοβηθεὶς Ἰωσὴφ παρέλαβεν αὐτὴν εἰς τήρησιν. καὶ εἶπεν αὐτῇ: Μαρία, ἰδοὺ παρέλαβόν σε ἐκ ναοῦ κυρίου τοῦ θεοῦ μου καὶ νῦν καταλιμπάνω σε ἐν τῷ οἴκῳ μου, ἀπέρχομαι γὰρ οἰκοδομῆσαι τὰς οἰκοδομάς μου, καὶ ἐν τάχει ἥξω πρὸς σέ. κύριος ὁ θεὸς διαφυλάξει σε.

10

1 Ἐγένετο δὲ συμβούλιον τῶν ἱερέων λεγόντων: ποιήσωμεν καταπέτασμα τῷ ναῷ κυρίου. καὶ εἶπεν ὁ ἱερεύς: καλέσατέ μοι ὧδε ἑπτὰ παρθένους ἀμιάντους ἐκ φυλῆς Δαυίδ. καὶ ἀπῆλθον οἱ ὑπηρέται καὶ εὕρησαν ἑπτά (εὗρον ἕξ). καὶ ἐμνήσθη ὁ ἱερεύς, ὅτι Μαρία ἐκ φυλῆς Δαυίδ ἐστι καὶ ἀμίαντός ἐστιν. καὶ ἀπῆλθαν οἱ ὑπηρέται καὶ ἤγαγον αὐτήν. καὶ εἰσήγαγεν αὐτὰς ὁ ἱερεὺς ἐν τῷ ναῷ κυρίου καὶ εἶπεν: λάχετέ μοι ὧδε, τίς νήσει τὸ χρυσίον καὶ τὸ ἀμίαντον καὶ τὸ βύσσινον καὶ τὸ σηρικοῦν καὶ τὸ ὑάκινθον καὶ τὸ κόκκινον καὶ τὴν ἀληθινὴν πορφύραν. καὶ ἔλαχεν τὴν Μαριὰμ τὸ κόκκινον καὶ ἡ ἀληθινὴ πορφύρα. καὶ λαβοῦσα ἀπῆλθεν εἰς τὸν οἶκον αὐτῆς. τῷ δὲ καιρῷ ἐκείνῳ Ζαχαρίας ἐσίγησεν. Μαριὰμ δὲ λαβοῦσα τὸ κόκκινον ἔκλωσεν.

11

1 Καὶ λαβοῦσα κάλπιν ἐξῆλθεν γεμίσαι ὕδωρ, καὶ ἰδοὺ φωνὴ λέγουσα: χαῖρε κεχαριτωμένη, ὁ κύριος μετὰ σοῦ, εὐλογημένη σὺ ἐν γυναιξί. καὶ περιεβλέπετο δεξιὰ καὶ ἀριστερά, πόθεν αὕτη ἡ φωνὴ ὑπάρχει, καὶ ἔντρομος γενομένη ἀπῆλθεν εἰς τὸν οἶκον αὐτῆς. καὶ ἀναπαύσασα τὴν κάλπην ἔλαβε πάλιν τὴν πορφύραν καὶ ἐκάθισεν ἐπὶ τὸν θρόνον καὶ εἶλκεν αὐτήν. 2 καὶ ἰδοὺ ἄγγελος κυρίου ἐπέστη λέγων αὐτῇ: μὴ φοβοῦ, Μαριάμ, εὗρες γὰρ χάριν ἐνώπιον τοῦ θεοῦ καὶ συλλήψῃ ἐκ λόγου αὐτοῦ. ἀκούσασα δὲ Μαριὰμ διεκρίθη ἐν ἑαυτῇ λέγουσα: ἐγὼ συλλήψομαι, ὡς πᾶσα γυνὴ γεννᾷ; 3 καὶ λέγει πρὸς αὐτὴν ὁ ἄγγελος: οὐχ οὕτως, Μαριάμ: δύναμις γὰρ θεοῦ ἐπισκιάσει σοι, διὸ καὶ τὸ γεννόμενον (ἐκ σοῦ) ἅγιον κληθήσεται υἱὸς ὑψίστου,

καὶ καλέσεις τὸ ὄνομα αὐτοῦ Ἰησοῦν: αὐτὸς γὰρ σώσει τὸν λαὸν αὐτοῦ ἀπὸ τῶν ἁμαρτιῶν αὐτῶν. καὶ εἶπεν Μαριάμ: ἰδοὺ ἡ δούλη κυρίου: γένοιτό μοι κατὰ τὸ ῥῆμά σου.

12

1 Καὶ ἐποίησεν τὴν πορφύραν καὶ τὸ κόκκινον καὶ ἀπήνεγκεν αὐτὰ τῷ ἱερεῖ, καὶ εὐλόγησεν αὐτὴν ὁ ἱερεὺς καὶ εἶπεν: Μαριάμ, ἐμεγάλυνε κύριος ὁ θεὸς τὸ ὄνομά σου ἐν πάσαις ταῖς γενεαῖς τῆς γῆς καὶ ἔσῃ εὐλογημένη ὑπὸ κυρίου. **2** χαρὰν δὲ λαβοῦσα Μαριὰμ ἀπῆλθε πρὸς τὴν συγγενίδα αὐτῆς Ἐλισάβετ καὶ ἔκρουσε πρὸς τῇ θύρᾳ. καὶ ἀκούσασα Ἐλισάβετ ἔρριψε τὸ ἐν χερσὶν, καὶ δραμοῦσα ἤνοιξεν αὐτῇ καὶ εὐλόγησεν αὐτὴν καὶ εἶπεν: πόθεν μοι τοῦτο, ἵνα ἡ μήτηρ τοῦ κυρίου μου ἔλθῃ πρὸς ἐμέ; ἰδοὺ γὰρ τὸ ἐν ἐμοὶ βρέφος ἐσκίρτησε καὶ εὐλόγησέν σε. Μαριὰμ δὲ ἐπελάθετο τῶν μυστηρίων, ὧν εἶπεν πρὸς αὐτὴν Γαβριήλ, καὶ ἀτενίσασα εἰς τὸν οὐρανὸν εἶπεν: τίς εἰμι ἐγώ, ὅτι πᾶσαι αἱ γυναῖκες μακαριοῦσί με; **3** ἐποίησε δὲ τρεῖς μῆνας πρὸς τὴν Ἐλισάβετ καὶ ἀπῆλθεν εἰς τὸν οἶκον αὐτῆς. ἡμέρᾳ δὲ ἀφ' ἡμέρας ἡ γαστὴρ αὐτῆς ὀγκοῦτο, καὶ ἔκρυβεν ἑαυτὴν ἀπὸ τῶν υἱῶν Ἰσραήλ. ἦν δὲ ἐτῶν πεντεκαίδεκα, ὅτε τὰ μυστήρια ταῦτα ἐγένοντο.

13

1 Ἐγένετο δὲ ἕκτος μὴν καὶ ἦλθεν Ἰωσὴφ ἀπὸ τῶν οἰκοδομῶν αὐτοῦ καὶ εἰσῆλθεν ἐν τῷ οἴκῳ αὐτοῦ καὶ εὗρε τὴν Μαριὰμ ὀγκωμένην. καὶ ἔτυψε τὸ πρόσωπον αὐτοῦ καὶ ἔρριψεν ἑαυτὸν χαμαὶ καὶ ἔκλαυσε λέγων: ποίῳ προσόπῳ ἀτενίσω πρὸς κύριον τὸν θεόν μου; τί δὴ εἴπω περὶ τῆς κόρης ταύτης, ὅτι παρθένον αὐτὴν παρέλαβον ἐκ ναοῦ κυρίου καὶ οὐκ ἐφύλαξα αὐτήν; τίς ὁ θηρεύσας με; τίς τὸ πονηρὸν τοῦτο ἐποίησεν ἐν τῷ οἴκῳ μου καὶ ἐμίανεν τὴν παρθένον; μήτι εἰς ἐμὲ ἀνεκεφαλαιώθη ἡ ἱστορία Ἀδάμ; ὥσπερ γὰρ Ἀδὰμ ἦν ἐν τῇ ὥρᾳ τῆς δοξολογίας αὐτοῦ καὶ ἦλθεν ὁ ὄφις καὶ εὗρεν τὴν Εὔαν μόνην καὶ ἐξηπάτησεν αὐτήν, οὕτως κἀμοὶ συνέβη. **2** καὶ ἀνέστη Ἰωσὴφ ἀπὸ τοῦ σάκκου καὶ ἐκάλεσε τὴν Μαριὰμ καὶ εἶπεν αὐτῇ: μεμελημένη τῷ θεῷ, τί τοῦτο ἐποίησας; τί ἐταπείνωσας τὴν ψυχήν σου; ἐπελάθου κυρίου τοῦ θεοῦ σου, ἡ ἀνατραφεῖσα εἰς τὰ ἅγια τῶν ἁγίων καὶ

λαβοῦσα τροφὴν ἐκ χειρὸς ἀγγέλου καὶ χορεύσασα ἐν αὐτοῖς; 3
ἡ δὲ ἔκλαυσε πικρῶς λέγουσα: ζῇ κύριος ὁ θεός, καθότι καθαρά
εἰμι ἐγὼ καὶ ἄνδρα οὐ γινώσκω. εἶπε δὲ αὐτῇ Ἰωσήφ: πόθεν οὖν
ἐστι τοῦτο ἐν τῇ γαστρί σου; εἶπε δὲ αὐτῷ: ζῇ κύριος ὁ θεός μου,
καθότι οὐ γινώσκω, πόθεν ἐστὶ τοῦτο τὸ ἐν τῇ γαστρί μου.

14

1 Καὶ ἐφοβήθη Ἰωσὴφ σφόδρα καὶ ἠρέμησεν ἐξ αὐτῆς καὶ
διελογίζετο, τί αὐτὴν ποιήσει, εἶπε δὲ ἐν ἑαυτῷ: ἐὰν αὐτῆς
κρύψω τὸ ἀμάρτημα, εὑρεθήσομαι μαχόμενος τῷ νόμῳ κυρίου:
καὶ ἐὰν αὐτὴν φανερὰν ποιήσω τοῖς υἱοῖς Ἰσραήλ, φοβοῦμαι,
μήπως ἀγγελικόν ἐστι τὸ ἐν αὐτῇ καὶ εὑρεθήσομαι παραδιδοὺς
αἷμα ἀθῷον εἰς κρίμα θανάτου. τί οὖν αὐτὴν ποιήσω; λάθρα
αὐτὴν ἀπολύσω ἀπ' ἐμοῦ. καὶ ταῦτα αὐτοῦ ἐνθυμουμένου
κατέλαβεν αὐτὸν ἡ νύξ. 2 καὶ ἰδοὺ ἄγγελος κυρίου φαίνεται
αὐτῷ κατ' ὄναρ λέγων: Ἰωσήφ (υἱὸς Δαυίδ), μὴ φοβηθῇς τὴν
παῖδα ταύτην. τὸ γὰρ ἐν αὐτῇ γεννηθὲν ἐκ πνεύματός ἐστιν
ἁγίου, καὶ καλέσεις τὸ ὄνομα αὐτοῦ Ἰησοῦν: αὐτὸς γὰρ σώσει
τὸν λαὸν αὐτοῦ ἀπὸ τῶν ἁμαρτιῶν αὐτῶν. καὶ ἀνέστη Ἰωσὴφ
ἀπὸ τοῦ ὕπνου καὶ ἐδόξασε τὸν θεὸν Ἰσραὴλ τὸν δόντα αὐτῷ
τὴν χάριν ταύτην, καὶ ἐφύλασσε τὴν παῖδα.

15

1 Ἦλθεν δὲ Ἄννας ὁ γραμματεὺς πρὸς αὐτὸν καὶ εἶπεν αὐτῷ: διὰ
τί οὐκ ἐφάνης ἐν τῇ συναγωγῇ (συνόδῳ) ἡμῶν; καὶ εἶπεν αὐτῷ
Ἰωσήφ: ὅτι κεκμηκὼς ἤμην ἐκ τῆς ὁδοῦ καὶ ἀνεπαυσάμην
ἡμέραν μίαν . καὶ ἐστράφη Ἄννας καὶ εἶδεν τὴν παρθένον
ὀγκωμένην. 2 καὶ ἀπελθὼν δρομαίως πρὸς τὸν (ἀρχ-)ιερέα εἶπεν
αὐτῷ: Ἰωσήφ, ὃν σὺ μαρτυρεῖς, ἠνόμησε σφόδρα. καὶ εἶπεν ὁ
ἱερεύς: τί τοῦτο; καὶ εἶπεν Ἄννας: τὴν παρθένον, ἣν παρέλαβεν
ἐκ ναοῦ κυρίου, ἐμίανεν αὐτήν. καὶ ἀποκριθεὶς ὁ ἱερεὺς εἶπεν
αὐτῷ: Ἰωσήφ; Ἰωσήφ τοῦτο ἐποίησεν; καὶ εἶπεν Ἄννας:
ἀπόστειλον ὑπηρέτας καὶ εὑρέσεις τὴν παρθένον ὀγκωμένην.
καὶ ἀπῆλθον οἱ ὑπηρέται καὶ εὗρον αὐτήν, καθὼς εἶπεν, καὶ
ἀπήγαγον ἅμα τῷ Ἰωσὴφ εἰς τὸ κριτήριον. 3 καὶ εἶπεν ὁ ἱερεύς:
Μαριάμ, τί τοῦτο ἐποίησας καὶ ἐταπείνωσας τὴν ψυχήν σου καὶ
ἐπελάθου κυρίου τοῦ θεοῦ σου, ἡ ἀνατραφεῖσα εἰς τὰ ἅγια τῶν

ἁγίων καὶ λαβοῦσα τροφὴν ἐκ χειρὸς ἀγγέλων, σὺ ἡ ἀκούσασα τὸν ὕμνον αὐτῶν καὶ χορεύσασα ἐνώπιον αὐτῶν; τί τοῦτο ἐποίησας; ἡ δὲ ἔκλαυσε πικρῶς λέγουσα: ζῇ κύριος ὁ θεός, ὅτι καθαρά εἰμι ἐγὼ ἐνώπιον αὐτοῦ καὶ ἄνδρα οὐ γινώσκω. 4 καὶ εἶπεν ὁ ἀρχιερεύς: Ἰωσήφ, τί τοῦτο ἐποίησας; καὶ εἶπεν Ἰωσήφ: ζῇ κύριος ὁ θεός μου, ὅτι καθαρός εἰμι ἐξ αὐτῆς. καὶ εἶπεν ὁ ἀρχιερεύς: μὴ ψευδομαρτύρει, ἀλλὰ λέγε τὸ ἀληθές: ἔκλεψας τοὺς γάμους καὶ οὐκ ἐφανέρωσας τοῖς υἱοῖς Ἰσραήλ, καὶ οὐκ ἔκλινας τὴν κεφαλήν σου ὑπὸ τὴν κραταιὰν χεῖρα, ὅπως εὐλογηθῇ τὸ σπέρμα σου. καὶ Ἰωσὴφ ἐσίγησεν.

16

1 Καὶ εἶπεν ὁ ἱερεύς: ἀπόδος τὴν παρθένον, ἥν παρέλαβες ἐκ ναοῦ κυρίου. καὶ περίδακρυς γενόμενος ὁ Ἰωσὴφ ἔστη. καὶ εἶπεν ὁ ἱερεύς: ποτιῶ ὑμᾶς τὸ ὕδωρ τῆς ἐλέγξεως κυρίου καὶ φανερώσει τὰ ἁμαρτήματα ὑμῶν ἐν ὀφθαλμοῖς ὑμῶν. 2 καὶ λαβὼν ὁ ἱερεὺς ἐπότισε τὸν Ἰωσὴφ καὶ ἔπεμψεν αὐτὸν εἰς τὴν ὀρεινήν: καὶ ἦλθεν ὁλόκληρος. ἐπότισεν δὲ καὶ τὴν παρθένον καὶ ἔπεμψεν καὶ αὐτὴν εἰς τὴν ὀρεινήν: καὶ ἦλθεν ὁλόκληρος, καὶ ἐθαύμασε πᾶς ὁ λαός, ὅτι ἁμαρτία οὐχ εὑρέθη ἐν αὐτοῖς. 3 καὶ εἶπεν ὁ ἱερεύς: εἰ κύριος ὁ θεὸς οὐκ ἐφανέρωσεν τὴν ἁμαρτίαν ὑμῶν, οὐδὲ ἐγὼ κρίνω ὑμᾶς καὶ ἀπέλυσεν αὐτούς. καὶ παρέλαβεν Ἰωσὴφ τὴν Μαριὰμ καὶ ἀπίει εἰς τὸν οἶκον αὐτοῦ χαίρων καὶ δοξάζων τὸν θεὸν τοῦ Ἰσραήλ.

17

1 Κέλευσις δὲ ἐγένετο ἀπὸ (τοῦ Ἀόστου) Ἡρώδου τοῦ βασιλέως ἀπογράψασθαι, ὅσοι εἰσὶν ἐν Βηθλεὲμ τῆς Ἰουδαίας. (ἠναγκάζετο δὲ Ἰωσὴφ ἀπελθεῖν ἐκ Ναζαρὲτ εἰς τὴν Βηθλεὲμ καὶ εἶπεν) καὶ εἶπεν Ἰωσήφ: ἐγὼ ἀπογράψομαι τοὺς υἱούς μου. ταύτην δὲ τὴν παῖδα τί ποιήσω; πῶς αὐτὴν ἀπογράψομαι; γυναῖκα ἐμήν; ἐπαισχύνομαι. ἀλλὰ θυγατέρα; οἶδαν οἱ υἱοὶ Ἰσραήλ, ὅτι οὐκ ἔστιν θυγάτηρ μου. αὐτὴ ἡ ἡμέρα Κυρίου ποιήσει, ὡς βούλεται. 2 καὶ ἔστρωσεν τὸν ὄνον, καὶ ἐκάθισεν αὐτὴν καὶ ἦλκεν ὁ υἱὸς αὐτοῦ καὶ ἠκολούθησεν Σαμουήλ (αὐτός). καὶ ἤγγισαν ἐπὶ μίλιον τρίτον, καὶ ἐστράφη Ἰωσὴφ καὶ εἶδεν αὐτὴν στυγνὴν καὶ ἔλεγεν: ἴσως τὸ ἐν αὐτῇ χειμάζει αὐτήν.

καὶ πάλιν ἐστράφη Ἰωσὴφ καὶ εἶδεν αὐτὴν γελοῦσαν καὶ εἶπεν:
Μαριάμμη, τί ἐστίν σοι τοῦτο, ὅτι τὸ πρόσωπόν σου βλέπω ποτὲ
μὲν γελοῦντα ποτὲ δὲ στυγνάζον; καὶ εἶπεν αὐτῷ: Ἰωσήφ, ὅτι
δύο λαοὺς βλέπω ἐν τοῖς ὀφθαλμοῖς μου, ἕνα κλαίοντα καὶ
κοπτόμενον καὶ ἕνα χαίροντα καὶ ἀγαλλιῶντα. 3 καὶ ἤλθωσεν
ἀνὰ μέσον τῆς ὁδοῦ, καὶ εἶπεν αὐτῷ Μαριάμμη: κατάγαγέ με
ἀπὸ τοῦ ὄνου, ὅτι (τ)ὸ ἐν ἐμοὶ ἐπείγει με προελθεῖν. καὶ
κατήγαγεν αὐτὴν ἐκεῖ καὶ εἶπεν αὐτῇ: ποῦ σε ἀπάξω καὶ
σκεπάσω σου τὴν ἀσχημοσύνην, ὅτι ὁ τόπος ἔρημός ἐστιν;

18

1 Καὶ εὗρεν ἐκεῖ σπήλαιον καὶ εἰσήγαγεν αὐτὴν καὶ παρέστησεν
αὐτῇ τοὺς υἱοὺς αὐτοῦ καὶ ἐξῆλθεν ζητῆσαι μαῖαν (Ἑβραίαν) ἐν
χώρᾳ Βηθλεέμ. 2 ἐγὼ δὲ Ἰωσὴφ περιεπάτουν καὶ οὐ
περιεπάτουν. καὶ ἀνέβλεψα εἰς τὸν πόλον τοῦ οὐρανοῦ καὶ εἶδον
αὐτὸν ἐστῶτα, καὶ εἰς τὸν ἀέρα καὶ εἶδον αὐτὸν ἔκθαμβον, καὶ
τὰ πετεινὰ τοῦ οὐρανοῦ ἠρεμοῦντα. καὶ ἐπέβλεψα ἐπὶ τὴν γῆν
καὶ εἶδον σκάφην κειμένην καὶ ἐργάτας ἀνακειμένους, καὶ ἦσαν
αἱ χεῖρες αὐτῶν ἐν τῇ σκάφῃ. καὶ οἱ μασόμενοι οὐκ ἐμασῶντο,
καὶ οἱ αἴροντες οὐκ ἀνέφερον, καὶ οἱ προσφέροντες τῷ στόματι
αὐτῶν οὐ προσέφερον. ἀλλὰ πάντων ἦν τὰ πρόσωπα ἄνω
βλέποντα. 3 καὶ εἶδον ἐλαυνόμενα πρόβατα, καὶ τὰ πρόβατα
ἐστήκει: καὶ ἐπῆρεν ὁ ποιμὴν τὴν χεῖρα αὐτοῦ τοῦ πατάξαι αὐτά,
καὶ ἡ χεὶρ αὐτοῦ ἔστη ἄνω. καὶ ἀνέβλεψα ἐπὶ τὸν χείμαρρον τοῦ
ποταμοῦ καὶ εἶδον ἐρίφους καὶ τὰ στόματα αὐτῶν ἐπικείμενα
τῷ ὕδατι καὶ μὴ πίνοντα. καὶ πάντα ὑπὸ θῆξιν (θήζει, θίζει,
θρίζιν, ἔκπληξιν) τῷ δρόμῳ ἀπηλαύνοντο.

19

1 Καὶ εἶδον γυναῖκα καταβαίνουσαν ἀπὸ τῆς ὀρεινῆς καὶ εἶπέν
μοι: ἄνθρωπε, ποῦ πορεύῃ; καὶ εἶπον αὐτῇ: μαῖαν ζητῶ. καὶ
ἀποκριθεῖσά μοι εἶπεν: ἐξ Ἰσραήλ; καὶ εἶπον αὐτῇ: ναί, κυρία. καὶ
εἶπέν μοι: τίς ἐστιν ἡ γεννήσασα ἐν τῇ σπηλαίῳ; καὶ εἶπον ἐγώ: ἡ
μεμνηστευμένη μοι. καὶ εἶπέν μοι: οὐκ ἔστι σου γυνή; καὶ εἶπον
αὐτῇ: Μαριάμ ἐστιν καὶ ἐκληρωσάμην αὐτὴν εἰς γυναῖκα, ἥτις
ἀνετράφη εἰς τὰ ἅγια τῶν ἁγίων: καὶ οὐκ ἔστι μου γυνή, ἀλλὰ
σύλληψιν ἔχει ἐκ πνεύματος ἁγίου. καὶ εἶπεν: εἰπέ μοι τὸ ἀληθές.

καὶ εἶπον αὐτῇ: ἐλθὲ καὶ ἴδε. καὶ ἀπῆλθεν μετ' αὐτοῦ. **2** καὶ ἔστη
ἐν τῷ τόπῳ τοῦ σπηλαίου, καὶ ἦν νεφέλη ἐπισκιάζουσα ἐπὶ τὸ
σπήλαιον: καὶ εἶπεν ἡ μαῖα: ἐμεγαλύνθη ἡ ψυχή μου τῇ σήμερον
ἡμέρᾳ, ὅτι εἶδον καινὸν θέαμα καὶ παράδοξον: ὅτι σωτηρίον τῷ
Ἰσραὴλ ἐγενήθη. καὶ παραχρῆμα ἡ νεφέλη ὑπεστέλλετο ἐκ τοῦ
σπηλαίου, καὶ ἐφάνη φῶς μέγα ἐν τῷ σπηλαίῳ, ὥστε τοὺς
ὀφθαλμοὺς ἡμῶν μὴ φέρειν. καὶ πρὸς ὀλίγον τὸ φῶς ἐκεῖνο
ὑπεστέλλετο, ἕως ἐφάνη τὸ βρέφος (καὶ ἦλθεν) καὶ ἔλαβεν
μασθὸν ἐκ τῆς μητρὸς αὐτοῦ Μαρίας. (καὶ ἀνεβόησεν ἡ μαῖα: ὡς
μεγάλη ἡ σήμερον ἡμέρα, ὅτι εἶδον τὸ καινὸν θέαμα τοῦτο.) **3**
καὶ ἐξῆλθεν ἐκ τοῦ σπηλαίου ἡ μαῖα καὶ ἀπήντησεν Σαλώμην,
καὶ εἶπεν αὐτῇ: Σαλώμη, Σαλώμη, καινόν σοι ἔχω διηγήσασθαι
θέαμα: παρθένος ἐγέννησεν, ὃ οὐ χωρεῖ φύσις ἀνθρωπίνη. καὶ
εἶπεν Σαλώμη: ζῇ κύριος ὁ θεός, ἐὰν μὴ κατανοήσω (ἐὰν μὴ
βάλω τὴν χεῖρά μου εἰς αὐτήν), οὐ μὴ πιστεύσω, ὅτι παρθένος
ἐγέννησεν.

20

1 Καὶ εἰσῆλθεν Σαλώμη καὶ εἶπεν: Μαρία, σχημάτισον σεαυτήν:
οὐ γὰρ μικρὸς ἀγὼν περίκειται περὶ σοῦ. καὶ κατενόησεν αὐτήν.
καὶ ἠλάλαξεν Σαλώμη καὶ ἐκραύγασε λέγουσα: οὐαὶ τῇ ἀνομίᾳ
μου καὶ οὐαὶ τῇ ἀπιστίᾳ μου, ὅτι ἐξεπείρασα θεὸν ζῶντα: καὶ
ἰδοὺ ἡ χείρ μου ἐν πυρὶ φλέγεται (ἀποπίπτει). **2** καὶ ἔκλινεν τὰ
γόνατα αὐτῆς Σαλώμη πρὸς τὸν δεσπότην λέγουσα: ὁ θεὸς τῶν
πατέρων μου, μνήσθητί μου, ὅτι σπέρμα εἰμὶ Ἀβραὰμ καὶ Ἰσαὰκ
καὶ Ἰακώβ: μὴ παραδειγματίσῃς με τοῖς υἱοῖς Ἰσραήλ, ἀλλὰ
ἀπόδος μοι ἐμὴν ὁλοκληρίαν. **3** καὶ ἰδοὺ ἄγγελος κυρίου ἔστη
πρὸς Σαλώμην λέγων: Σαλώμη, Σαλώμη, ἐπήκουσε κύριος ὁ θεὸς
τῆς δεήσεός σου: ἔγγισον πρὸς τὸ παιδίον καὶ βάστασον αὐτό,
καὶ ἔσται σοι σωτηρία μεγάλη. **4** καὶ προσῆλθεν Σαλώμη καὶ
ἐβάστασεν αὐτό, καὶ εἶπεν: ὄντως βασιλεὺς μέγας ἐγεννήθη τῷ
Ἰσραήλ. καὶ εὐθέως ἰάθη Σαλώμη καὶ ἐξῆλθεν ἐκ τοῦ σπηλαίου
δεδικαιωμένη, καὶ ἰδοὺ φωνὴ λέγουσα αὐτῇ: Σαλώμη, Σαλώμη,
μὴ ἀναγγείλῃς, ὅσα εἶδες παράδοξα (ἕως ἔλθῃ εἰς Ἰερουσαλήμ).

21

1 Καὶ ἰδοὺ Ἰωσὴφ ἡτοιμάσθη ἐξελθεῖν εἰς τὴν Ἰουδαίαν, καὶ θόρυβος ἐγένετο ἐν Βηθλεέμ. ἦλθαν γὰρ μάγοι ἀπὸ ἀνατολῶν (ἐκ Περσίδος) λέγοντες: ποῦ ἔστιν ὁ τεχθεὶς βασιλεὺς τῶν Ἰουδαίων; εἴδομεν γὰρ αὐτοῦ τὸν ἀστέρα ἐν τῇ ἀνατολῇ καὶ ἤλθομεν προσκυνῆσαι αὐτόν. 2 καὶ ἀκούσας Ἡρώδης ἐταράχθη καὶ ἔπεμψεν ὑπηρέτας πρὸ(ς) τοὺς μάγους, καὶ ἀπέστειλεν πρὸς τοὺς ἀρχιερεῖς καὶ ἀνέκρινεν αὐτοὺς λέγων: ποῦ ὁ χριστὸς γεννᾶται; οἱ δὲ εἶπον: ἐν Βηθλεὲμ τῆς Ἰουδαίας: οὕτως γὰρ γέγραπται. καὶ ἀπέλυσεν αὐτοὺς καὶ ἀνέκρινε τοὺς μάγους λέγων αὐτοῖς: τί εἴδετε σημεῖον ἐπὶ τὸν γεννηθέντα βασιλέα; καὶ εἶπον οἱ μάγοι: εἴδομεν ἀστέρα παμμεγέθη λάμψαντα ἐν τοῖς ἄστροις τούτοις καὶ ἀμβλύνοντα αὐτοὺς τοῦ (μὴ) φαίνειν καὶ ἔγνωμεν, ὅτι βασιλεὺς ἐγεννήθη τῷ Ἰσραήλ: καὶ διὰ τοῦτο ἤλθομεν προσκυνῆσαι αὐτόν. καὶ εἶπεν Ἡρώδης: πορευθέντες ἀκριβῶς ἐκζητήσατε περὶ τοῦ παιδίου: καὶ ἐπὰν εὕρηται, ἀπαγγείλατέ μοι, ὅπως κἀγὼ ἐλθὼν προσκυνήσω αὐτόν. 3 καὶ ἐξῆλθον οἱ μάγοι, καὶ ἰδοὺ ὁ ἀστήρ, ὃν εἶδον ἐν τῇ ἀνατολῇ, προῆγεν αὐτῶν, ἕως οὗ ἐλθὼν ἔστη εἰς τὸ σπήλαιον ἐπὶ τῆς κεφαλῆς τοῦ παιδίου. καὶ ἰδόντες αὐτὸ οἱ μάγοι μετὰ τῆς μητρὸς αὐτοῦ Μαρίας προσεκύνησαν αὐτὸ καὶ ἀνοίξαντες τοὺς θησαυροὺς αὐτῶν προσήνεγκαν αὐτῶν δῶρα, χρυσὸν καὶ λίβανον καὶ σμύρναν. καὶ χρηματισθέντες ὑπὸ ἁγίου ἀγγέλου (μὴ εἰσελθεῖν εἰς τὴν Ἰουδαίαν πρὸς Ἡρώδην) δι' ἄλλης ὁδοῦ ἐπορεύθησαν εἰς τὴν χώραν αὐτῶν.

22

1 Γνοὺς δὲ ὁ Ἡρώδης, ὅτι ἐνεπαίχθη ὑπὸ τῶν μάγων, ὀργισθεὶς ἔπεμψεν τοὺς φονευτὰς κελεύσας αὐτοῖς ἀνελεῖν τὰ βρέφη ἀπὸ διετοῦς καὶ κατωτέρω. 2 ἀκούσασα δὲ Μαριάμ, ὅτι τὰ βρέφη ἀναιροῦνται, φοβηθεῖσα ἔλαβεν τὸ παιδίον μετὰ Ἰωσὴφ καὶ ἀπεδήμησεν εἰς Αἴγυπτον, καθὼς ἐχρηματίσθη αὐτοῖς. 3 ἡ δὲ Ἐλισάβετ λαβοῦσα τὸν Ἰωάννην ἀνέβη εἰς τὴν ὀρεινὴν καὶ περιεβλέπετο, ποῦ αὐτὸν ἀποκρύψει: καὶ οὐκ ἦν αὐτοῖς τόπος ἀποκρυβῆς. τότε στενάξασα λέγει: ὄρος, ὄρος, δέξαι μητέρα μετὰ τέκνου . οὐ γὰρ ἠδύνατο πορεύεσθαι. καὶ παραχρῆμα ἐδιχάσθη τὸ ὄρος καὶ ἐδέξατο αὐτήν. καὶ ἦν τὸ ὄρος ἐκεῖνο διαφαῖνον αὐτοῖς καὶ ἄγγελος κυρίου ὁδηγῶν αὐτούς.

23

1 Ὁ δὲ Ἡρώδης ἐζήτει τὸν Ἰωάννην καὶ ἀπέστειλεν ὑπηρέτας εἰς τὸ θυσιαστήριον κυρίου πρὸς Σαχαρίαν λέγων: ποῦ ἀπέκρυψας τὸν υἱόν σου; ὁ δὲ εἶπεν αὐτοῖς: ἐγὼ λειτουργὸς ὑπάρχω κυρίου τοῦ θεοῦ καὶ παρεδρεύω τῷ ναῷ αὐτοῦ καὶ οὐ γινώσκω, ποῦ ἐστιν ὁ υἱός μου. 2 οἱ δὲ ὑπηρέται πορευθέντες ἀνήγγειλαν τῷ Ἡρώδῃ. καὶ ὀργισθεὶς ὁ Ἡρώδης ἀπέστειλεν ἐκ δευτέρου πρὸς Σαχαρίαν λέγων: εἰπέ μοι τὸ ἀληθές, ποῦ ἐστιν ὁ υἱός σου: οἶδας γάρ, ὅτι τὸ αἷμά σου ὑπὸ τὴν χεῖρά μού ἐστιν. οἱ δὲ ὑπηρέται ἀπῆλθον καὶ ἀνήγγειλαν τῷ Σαχαρίᾳ ταῦτα. 3 καὶ εἶπεν αὐτοῖς ὁ Σαχαρίας: εἴπατε τῷ Ἡρώδῃ: εἰ καὶ τὸ αἷμά μου ἐκχέεις, τὸ πνεῦμά μου ὁ δεσπότης λήψεται, πλὴν ὅτι ἀθῷον αἷμα ἐκχύνεις παρὰ τὰ πρόθυρα τοῦ ναοῦ κυρίου. οὐ γὰρ γινώσκω, ποῦ ἐστιν ὁ υἱός μου. καὶ περὶ τὸ διάφαυμα ἐφονεύθη Σαχαρίας. καὶ οὐκ ᾔδεισαν οἱ υἱοὶ Ἰσραήλ, πῶς ἐφονεύθη.

24

1 Ἀλλὰ τῇ ὥρᾳ τοῦ ἀσπασμοῦ ἀπῆλθον οἱ ἱερεῖς, καὶ οὐκ ἀπήντησεν αὐτοῖς ὁ Σαχαρίας κατὰ τὸ εἰωθός, καὶ ἔστησαν οἱ ἱερεῖς προσδοκῶντες τὸν Σαχαρίαν τοῦ ἀσπάσασθαι αὐτὸν ἐν εὐχαῖς καὶ δοξάσαι τὸν θεόν. 2 χρονίσαντος δὲ αὐτοῦ ἐφοβήθησαν ἅπαντες. ἀποτολμήσας δὲ εἷς ἐξ αὐτῶν εἰσῆλθεν καὶ εἶδεν παρὰ τὸ θυσιαστήριον κυρίου αἷμα πεπηγός. καὶ ἰδοὺ φωνὴ λέγουσα: Σαχαρίας πεφόνευται καὶ οὐκ ἐξαλειφθήσεται τὸ αἷμα αὐτοῦ, ἕως οὗ ἔλθῃ ὁ ἔκδικος αὐτοῦ. ὁ δὲ ἀκούσας τὸν λόγον τοῦτον ἐφοβήθη καὶ ἐλθὼν ἀνήγγειλε τοῖς ἱερεῦσιν, ἃ εἶδεν καὶ ἤκουσεν. 3 καὶ τολμήσαντες εἰσῆλθον καὶ εἶδον τὸ γεγονός. καὶ τὰ δὲ φατνώματα τοῦ ναοῦ ὀλόλυξαν, καὶ αὐτοὶ διεσχίσαντο τὰ ἱμάτια αὐτῶν ἀπὸ ἄνωθεν ἕως κάτω. τὸ δὲ σῶμα αὐτοῦ οὐχ εὗρον, ἀλλ' εὗρον τὸ αἷμα αὐτοῦ ὡσεὶ λίθον γεγενημένον. ἐξελθόντες δὲ ἀνήγγειλαν τῷ λαῷ ὅτι Σαχαρίας πεφόνευται. καὶ ἤκουσαν πᾶσαι αἱ φυλαὶ τοῦ λαοῦ καὶ ἐπένθησαν αὐτὸν τρεῖς ἡμέρας καὶ τρεῖς νύκτας. 4 μετὰ δὲ τὰς ἡμέρας ἐκείνας ἐβουλεύσαντο οἱ ἱερεῖς, τίνα ἀναστήσωσιν εἰς τὸν τόπον Σαχαρίου, καὶ ἔβαλον κλήρους: καὶ ἔπεσεν ὁ κλῆρος ἐπὶ Συμεῶνα. αὐτὸς γὰρ ἦν χρηματισθεὶς ὑπὸ τοῦ ἁγίου

πνεύματος τοῦ μὴ ἰδεῖν θάνατον, ἕως ἄν ἴδῃ τὸν χριστὸν κυρίου (ἐν σαρκί).

Ἐγὼ δὲ Ἰάκωβος ἔγραψα τὴν ἱστορίαν ταύτην ἐν Ἰερουσαλήμ, καὶ ἐδόξασα τὸν δεσπότην θεὸν τὸν ἀποκαλύψαντα ἡμῖν τὰ μυστήρια ταῦτα. 2 ὅτι αὐτῷ πρέπει δόξα, κράτος εἰς τοὺς αἰῶνας τῶν αἰώνων, ἀμήν.

www.ingramcontent.com/pod-product-compliance
Lightning Source LLC
Chambersburg PA
CBHW070944120626
46546CB00004B/1558